"NO, I'M NOT STARVING"

(AN ARTIST'S JOURNEY)

BY GORDON HAAS

DEDICATION

To my parents, Ruth and Arthur Haas,
whose love and support will always be treasured.

ACKNOWLEDGMENTS

Christine Zdepski Haas (Kiki)
whose patience & understanding while editing made the
completion of this book possible.

To all the art teachers over the years,
especially Mrs. Hugg, 7th & 8th grade,
Nick Palermo, David Niles, Chris Van Allsburg
and all the other great RISD professors.

Most of all, my Uncle Hamilton Young, who bequeathed to me at the
age of twelve his art supplies, books, and spirit on how to love art.

1 PREPARATION

Prepping for a plein-air painting trip to Positano, Italy. Christine and I are off for another six weeks with my easel, paints, panels and all the little stuff needed to create about sixty oil paintings. I must not forget Chongo, our little Chihuahua mix. He is a rescue dog we got just a little while ago. Some idiots in West Virginia threw the poor guy out like he was a piece of garbage. Well, now he's going to go to the Amalfi Coast, Positano, Capri and Ravello. I guess the little fellow is going to get some sweet revenge. Those morons probably haven't even made it out of their own back yard.

I first heard of the Amalfi Coast from folks coming into my

gallery and seeing paintings from Europe and talking about their trips. I often write down their suggestions to check out later. Positano and the Amalfi Coast kept coming up over and over again. I then started to check it out for the possibility of a painting trip. I spend quite a bit of time going over our travel books and checking out Google Earth and talking in great detail to people at the gallery. We have already done Montalcino in Tuscany and were considering a number of locations, possibly Lake Cuomo, Venice or back to Tuscany. Italy wasn't the only possibility. Ireland and Greece are definitely on our short list. As a painter, I try to find places that are different than I've painted before. I want to stretch myself and try different things. For years now I've been painting the Bucks County area. I love it here with the river, canal, beautiful farms, street scenes and an endless supply of subject matter especially due to the changing seasons. I've often painted at the same location numerous times. That may sound boring to some; however, by the time I start getting tired of the colors the season is changing again. The greens of summer give way to the rich colors of fall, then the solitude of winter moves in, and before you know it the rebirth of the process starts all over again. Exploring the same location actually frees one up. You've dealt with the compositional issues before, the lighting, colors, etc. Now I'm free to paint -- really paint my heart out.

Ok, I've got the scale, the luggage bags, art supplies, clothes and all the stuff for a plein air painting trip. I've got fifty pounds per bag. I lament that a few years ago it was eighty pounds a bag. It was so easy back then. First I have to figure out how many tubes of paint to bring. Fortunately with my color theory, I paint with only six colors plus white and burnt umber to kill color. It's such a guessing game on how much to bring. I can't imagine being an artist who uses tons of different colors. I wouldn't know where to start. Let's see, I only use the large tubes, 150 ml. Maybe six tubes of white, lots of blue -- after all, we are going to be on the Mediterranean! Yes, lots of warm blue, say three tubes of cerulean and for my cool, three tubes of cobalt. Then my complimentary under painting for blue is orange; this means yellow and red. Cadmium yellow and cadmium red are my warm, say two tubes of each.

Now I need my cool yellow and cool red -- that's yellow ochre and alizarin crimson. I know I always go through a lot of yellow ochre since I also use it for the quick gesture to start every painting, say maybe three tubes. Alizarin crimson is powerful stuff. A little dab will do ya, one tube. That leaves burnt umber. I only use a bit of it to soften and dull colors when they are too intense. Wait a minute, sixty paintings -- I did forty-four in Tuscany last year but I'm bringing smaller panels. I guess I should bring about the same amount of paint -- no, I'm painting thicker -- or as Christine says, "globbier." Add one tube of each color and hopefully I have the right amount of paints.

Here they go on the scale in their plastic boxes. I'm trying to avoid an absolute mess in case any tube gets crushed, punctured or whatever. Thirty-seven pounds of paint. This is going to be interesting. There are four bags between us which are a total of two-hundred pounds. My carry on is my half box Julian easel. Christine's carry on is her personal stuff. One bag at fifty pounds is the largest panels wrapped up in a cardboard box I make with luggage straps holding it together. That leaves one-hundred fifty pounds for all the rest of the smaller panels, the paints and other art supplies I need: palette, brushes, rags et cetera. Plus all our clothes, hair dryer, shoes and, of course, Chongo's stuff. This is going to take a while to make this work. One-hundred fifty pounds sounds like a lot but it disappears very quickly.

We get Chongo off to the vet. It is a fairly simple process to get him into Italy. In Italy, dogs are family. We already have his pet passport. His microchip, in case he gets lost, was implanted from his previous trip. He is all up to date with his various shots. All Italy cares about is the rabies shot. Even though Italy is in the EU, pet transport is different in each country. France and Great Britain have quarantine periods, as do some of the northern European countries. Italy seems to be one of the more relaxed. As I said, dogs are family. When in Italy, we take Chongo into the grocery store and he even eats at the restaurants on my lap. If we arrive at a restaurant without him, the owners always inquire about him and are disappointed if he is not with us. We explain that he is tired and sleeping. They understand but are visibly disappointed.

I have about a week to go. I've got to make endless phone calls to the credit card companies giving them the dates for the trip. If their computers see "unusual activity" they cut you off. There is nothing worse than trying to pay a bill with a card that you have all the room in the world on and, "What do you mean the card won't work?" I've got to let my bank know the dates or the same thing will happen to the ATM card -- details, details, details.

I still have to get all the envelopes together for Donna, my gallery director. Thank goodness she's my sister-in-law, Christine's sister. I get her pay checks all dated for each week, then checks for electric, phone, rent, vendors and always some blank checks all signed by me for the unexpected -- there's always the unexpected.

The house -- first and foremost, the mortgage, and then the envelopes with checks for Donna to walk over to the bank, plus withdrawal and deposit slips to transfer money as needed to cover any checks. We don't want any checks going bounce, bounce, bounce. When we leave for the airport, I always shut off all the electric to the house at the fuse box except the circuit that goes to the refrigerator. I've got all kinds of homemade tomato sauce and pesto in the freezer that I make from scratch. We get the ingredients from our garden and the organic farm we are members of.

That's one thing from all of our trips to France and Italy is the love of real food. There's none of the Styrofoam Saran wrapped junk from the mega grocery store. Just give me some fish caught a few hours ago with veggies and fruit all picked that morning from Farmer Joe -- or should I say, Giuseppe. The season changes and the food changes. Whatever is fresh that day is your meal. It's that simple.

I've forgotten something -- I know I have. That's the irony with forgetting something. You can't remember what it is, so it's forgotten. On our first trip for my exhibition in Laon, France I didn't forget a thing. Perfect! We went on the trip, got home, went down to the gallery and had a great first day back. I downloaded all of my photographs -- ah, what great memories. My truck was parked a few blocks from the gallery. I left it there the morning of our trip. Donna picked us up at the gallery to take us to the airport. It's free parking on the street with no meters. That freaking street sweeper! I got a ticket for each week gone plus a nasty note from one of the residents on the street. Something about how the hell are they supposed to get their groceries in their house with me clogging up the parking -- oops, I knew I forgot something.

I'm still kind of surprised how well our first plein-air

painting trip to Tuscany went. We went through Montalcino twice on our first trip to Italy. We spent two days there early in the trip between Rome and Siena, and then we went onto Florence, Venice and back down to Cortona. Cortona, that's the little town in the book "Under the Tuscan Sun." We winged it for a place to stay. We do that a lot, just winging it.

My brother thinks I'm a little nuts but I think it makes it more of an adventure. We didn't really plan to travel that way, but it started on our first trip to France. The first five days were spent in Laon for my exhibit with day trips to Reims then up to the rolling hills at the Belgium border roaming the countryside -- oh, and Giverny, have to go there. We then went to the Loire Valley and finishing up in Paris.

After Cortona, Italy, Christine and I decided to skip Umbria for now and go back to Montalcino. We knew we were going to love it. Let's just spend a couple of days there and really get to know it. After a few days the decision was made that we will have to come back for an extended painting trip.

I'm a lucky guy, Christine leaves all trip planning to me.

She just says, "Take me." She doesn't want to have to think about anything except going along for the ride and enjoying it -- that is, until Positano. I think she's addicted. It's almost like a drug for her. When we came back last spring from the six-week painting trip, she definitely had withdrawal symptoms. It took her some time to recover. I don't think she ever totally will.

2 MONTALCINO, TUSCANY

The plane ride, customs, get the car, the drive, I'm tired. We used an online service for our little villa. It's a stand-alone villa with just three rooms like the local Italians really live with a living room, a kitchen, a bedroom and a bath. It also had a large patio with a picnic table. It is situated in the middle of olive groves and vineyards. Perfect. Now we are on the drive from Route Two, up through vineyards and olive groves about to find out if the villa is what was advertised or if we are about to get the surprise of our life. I follow the directions. "From the road just below the circle, take the dirt road between the cypress trees" -- I think to myself, "Are you kidding?" -- "down the dirt road through the vineyards and on the right you will see the sign "Greppini." Go down the dirt drive to the little villa."

We stop at the top of the drive and I say to Christine, "That's my first painting tomorrow morning. Look at that estate, it's incredible." We arrive at Greppini, a little stand alone casa down a dirt path generously called a "driveway." We pull up tired and excited. There's an elderly couple doing the final clean up, mopping the floors and getting it ready for their new guests. In my extremely poor Italian and his non-existent English, we went over the details of the electric and gas meter. Typically you pay separately for utilities when renting a house or apartment by the week. We each write down the meter readings on pieces of paper, which we will do again at the end of our stay and pay for what we used. The quaint little Italian couple goes on their way. We are alone with our solitude, time for siesta. We take a well deserved afternoon nap.

Now it's Saturday afternoon. Time to walk into town. I get out the map and decide on a route south of our villa around the circle and up into town. We get about half way to town and the shoulder on the road disappears. The traffic is whizzing by and we have no room to walk and a ten-foot high wall next to us. It gets scary. We turn around. We arrive back at the villa, take a breather, and I comb the map for another route. Christine is a huge walker. In her youth she ran spring track, running the half mile, mile and two mile and attended the Penn relays. In the fall she also ran varsity cross-country all four years in high school. Winter track was also in the repertoire. She has continued to run/walk, go to the gym and practice yoga for many years. She is a real athlete. Recently during an annual physical at the age of forty-three, her blood pressure came in at 97/55.

Christine doesn't have a very good sense of direction. I'm trying to find a route for her to walk in the morning. Christine walks about six miles. I need to find a route she can do on her own while I'm out painting where she doesn't get lost.

There is only one other way to possibly walk into town. I'm a little skeptical. This road looks very busy. It's getting to be about dinner-time. We decide to drive into town and get a bite for dinner. I'm scoping out the ride for a walking route for Kiki -- that's her childhood nickname. While in town, we walk the little streets so common in these little hilltop villages. We stretch our legs, recover from the long flight and get acclimated. I don't even remember where we ate that night -- it doesn't mater -- we were just unwinding. We drove back to our little villa and I took note of all the local Italians walking the road. This is the Italian way. After a long dinner enjoying good food and family you take a stroll in the evening. This, I come to find, is the big difference between the Italian life and the life of Americans. The conversation is the focus, along with friends and family. Not talking at one another but communicating. I can just hear the conversations about the proper way to make the pesto or when is the best time for harvesting the olive groves. These are such earthy things to talk about, not the typical things conversed about in New Jersey. I finally found the path for Kiki to walk to and from town. Life is good.

Monday morning nine o'clock, that's the time the hardware store opens. I can't bring turpentine on the plane because it's flammable. In Montalcino, the hardware store is closed on the weekend. Every painting trip at nine o'clock on Monday morning, I'm standing in front of the hardware store waiting for them to open.

Trementina -- sounds simple. Ok. So they open. I go in and find the section with the paint thinners. This looks easy -- uh oh, I can't find the trementina. What do I do now? Ok. No problem. I try to explain to a man behind the counter what turpentine is. "Io ono artista, olio artista". He has a blank look on his face -- obvious, in any language. I try again in my crummy Italian. No luck. He tries to understand but looks baffled. I must have looked frustrated. Here I am in Tuscany eager to get started painting and not even able to get my turpentine. A British accent -- what a bella sound. A man about my age comes to the rescue. I come to find out he has lived in Montalcino for five years. He asks me what I'm looking for. He explains it to the owner and, presto, I have my turpentine and off I go.

I race back to our villa to get organized and am anxious to do my first painting. I haul all of my stuff up the dirt driveway. I'm walking past olive trees to get to the top of the drive to retrieve the view as when we first arrived the other day. I start to set up my easel, my paints, palette and brushes while listening to the local Italian music on the headphones. Perfect. I'm actually here all set up standing in front of this fabulous estate with the cypress trees, vineyards and rolling hills. Bella, bella, bella. I take a deep breath and let's see what I can do.

I paint away with the glimmering light, strong but familiar at the same time. I paint using the same color theories I use back home. The scene is very different. I've never painted vineyards, olive trees or cypress before. Four hours later, I'm all done with my first plein air painting done overseas.

Wow, first painting done. The light seems to be similar to Bucks County. It's the middle of May, springtime in Tuscany, and I'm comfortable. I feel good. I'm all set up now with six more weeks of painting time ahead of me.

It's evening time. We have a glass of wine on our patio, breathe deeply and unwind. Christine and I decide to walk into town to try the new path. She is a little nervous about doing it on her own. Off we go on a trial run up the drive past my painting spot to the right and up the dusty path. The path wanders through a small estate that is run down but kept nicely at the same time. It's a real working estate with vineyards, olive trees, chickens and gardens. We make a right on the main road into town. Later on we learn that it's one of three roads into town. It's a beautiful twenty-minute walk, the perfect distance. I'm relieved. Christine won't feel trapped in our villa. She can do her walk into town on her own, loop around and kick up the dust on the dirt paths through the vineyards. If you travel the back paths in Tuscany, you will kick up a lot of dust. Christine would later say that she feels like "Pig Pen" with the dust swirling all around her.

I'm back painting at the top of our driveway. I've painted four or five paintings so far. I'm now focusing on the actual vines. It's freaking hot. I should have set up about thirty feet behind my spot. Shade under a tall tree is a wonderful thing for a plein air painter. I'm looking at rows and rows of vineyards across a small valley onto a large estate that looks like it has been there for many centuries. The height of the cypress trees are breathtaking. They are the largest ones I've ever seen. They are all in parallel formation from the main road along the driveway up to their front door.

My painting starts out mainly in warm and cool reds, the opposite on the color wheel of the final green hue. After I've finished the first layer of the opposite color, the painting always looks a little strange. It makes sense when you see it but not when you look at the scene in front of you. Aesthetically it is like looking at the negative of a photograph.

Now I'm starting the "like" colors -- no, I don't own a tube of green paint. I mix them all. I need some warm green. Green is cadmium yellow, cerulean blue and a bit of white. The amount of each determines the intensity of color and whether the green is on the yellow side or the blue side. White is added to lighten it or make it more pale or pastel. I then add a touch of burnt umber to kill the intensity of color and create a darker value. It is simple and effective. This gives me everything I need for all color combinations, value and hue.

I'm about three quarters finished half way through the "like" color with the headphones on and an Italian radio station playing a mix of new and old Italian music -- how fitting. I sense someone. I look around and see a man on the stoop of a nice but rather unkempt little villa over my left shoulder. I wave politely. I hope he doesn't mind me painting here. I am on the other side of the dirt path between the vineyards. I don't think it's his property -- who knows.

I just go back to my painting. He's right behind me. Silent. I pull my headphones off and say in my poor attempt at Italian "Buona sera." He leans to the right inquisitively and says, "That's looking pretty good" in far better English than my Italian. I just start laughing. "I'm trying to work on my Italian and you just blew it." He laughs. We shake hands and introduce ourselves. His name is Ferdinando.

He then asks me if I know what I am painting. I tell him that, "I'm painting a beautiful estate -- obviously that's a loaded question. Why don't you tell me what I'm painting?" Ferdinando chuckles a little, partly laughing and partly surprised. "That's the Biondi Santi estate. It's one of the most important wineries in all of Italy. They are the inventors of Brunello de Montalcino."

I had no idea what he was talking about. "Really? You're kidding me." I guess he could tell by my expression that I was not very familiar. He then proceeds to give me the full blown history in great detail. I was expecting to get bored out of my mind with this. As the story went on, I think I must have been getting into the Italian lifestyle. The whole story intrigued me until the end. Ferdinando next asks if my wife and I would like a private tour of the winery. It turns out that Ferdinando is the son-in-law to Franco, the eighty-four-year-old owner and has worked for him for over twenty years. Ferdinando gets on the cell phone and -- presto, Friday afternoon, a private tour.

Our villa has turned out just perfect, such a relief. Christine can take her long walks through the countryside and up into town, back down the far side through the arched gate and down into the valley to the vineyards and olive groves.

I can simply walk out the front door and do paintings of olive groves or villas of the rolling hills in the distance. Some days I just jump in the rental car and roam around on the streets in the surrounding hills and pull over and paint. The pull over spots quickly appear on the sides of the winding roads. You have to be quick or you blow by them. I'll get out of the car and scope out the vista for the magical views for the next painting.

I'm just south of Castelenouvo -- that's about five miles south of Montalcino. There is a particular pull over just south of town before the hill drops down an incredible grade into the valley. This is, of course, what gives it such a great vista overlooking the valley with hills layered in the distance one after another while fading into the mist. Breathtaking. I stand there and find myself saying out loud, "Magnifico, magnifico." I said it a number of times shaking my head back and fourth. I shrug my shoulders, pop the hatch to the rental car, pull out the Julian easel and the rest of my supplies. I put on the Italian tunes and off I go -- it's playtime!

We first met our friend, Simone, the previous year on our first trip to Italy, the "run around trip." We were enjoying a morning stroll after our cappuccino in our favorite café. Christine was checking out the clothes and jewelry in one shop while I was meandering around. I came upon a gallery. I thought to myself, "Interesting Tuscan scenes, different than I've seen so far on the trip." There were mosaic paintings in what looks like oils. They were painted with flat brushes in dot patterns to create the entire image. I'm looking around the gallery and realize a fellow in the back is painting at a drafting table, brushes in hand. "Buongiorno, buongiorno" -- the customary greeting in the morning. I see a little handmade sign on the table, "We speak English." I smile and explain that we do exactly the same thing in the United States. He looks at me a little puzzled. "I have a gallery in the States. Io sono artista" -- (I am artist.) I then say in simple English, "Artist, gallery, sell my paintings." He gets it! His English is, I'm sure, better than my clumsy Italian. I sensed right away he's a very warm fellow. He had a nice manner about him, kind of quiet and contemplative at the same time.

We introduce ourselves and Simone begins to explain his work. There are other artists' work in the gallery besides his. This is the same as when I first opened my gallery, but after six months I got rid of them all and began to only show my work. Having other artists only confused the customers. I did the math and it was my work that was selling. People like to meet the artist. They have a connection to the work that they would not have otherwise at a regular retail gallery.

Simone explains that he has only been painting for three or four years. He opened the gallery less than a year ago and simply doesn't have the amount of work to fill the space. Simone then proudly shows me his wife's work, Silvia's beautiful little watercolors. The paintings are only about two by three inches. They are lovely scenes of the area. They have villas, churches, cypress trees and hilltop towns in them. As he shows me her watercolors, he explains that she is an architect by training. There is another connection between us! My father and brother are architects. My father had his own firm for over forty years and now my brother has one, too. Simone explains in his broken English, "Very difficult in Italy. Architects come all over world to be here. Only way get work is in old family firm many, many years. There is no money in architecture here. Silvia is changing career to become artista so make money."

I laugh to myself at how funny that sounds. I can't image a parent saying, "I want to send my son/daughter to art school to become a painter because there is no money in architecture." I tell Simone of my experiences and suggest that he turns the gallery, in time, to only his work and his wife's. I leave him my website address. We then shake hands like we've known each other for a lifetime and off I go.

A year passes and I'm on a plein air trip back to Montalcino. I walk into Simone's gallery. I see him just as if he never moved from last year behind his drafting table with brushes in hand. "I don't know if you remember me."

Simone replies, "Gordono," in his Italian accent. "I go to your website many, many times. You are real artista." I laugh and thank him. I see the changes in his gallery. "Yes, yes. I took your advice and the gallery is only I, Silvia -- and I also keep tapestry lady." I ask, "How is it working for you?" He replies, "Oh, much better. It is nice not to split money with other artista." He smiles. "How long you stay in Montalcino?"

I reply, "Christine and I are here for six weeks. This is a painting trip for me." Simone tells me he must talk to Silvia to find time to have us over for dinner. I respond, "You set the time and we will be there. Ciao!"

I decide the next day to do a painting in town instead of in the countryside for the first time. I pull into the north side of town to a place where there is free parking and not too far from the café I want to paint. It is a lengthy process finding a location to paint. I have an idea of exactly where I want to go. I call it "scoping time." I'll wander around the area I'm thinking of painting to see how the light is. It could be the perfect spot, just too early in the day light. Three o'clock, that's the time I need to be here. I make a mental note for a future painting. I find my painting spot. I know it when I see it, just like when you see a painting you love. You know it when you see it. You can't necessarily explain why you love it. It just hits you.

It's the same when you find the right painting spot you've been looking for and, bam, there it is right in front of you. The light is just right. The folks are all sitting in the café. The colors of the umbrellas are magnificent. The flowers in the planters are brilliant with their intense hue. It feels right -- that's the key. It has to feel just right. It's the same as when you see a painting that you love. It just feels right.

I start setting up across from the café in the main square under the archway between the columns. I get everything ready to start painting. Everything is all set. I crank up the tunes louder than I probably should. It's a bit noisy at the main piazza. I take a deep breath, focus. The gesture is the most important part of painting for me. It is just like drawing the figure at RISD. It takes one minute to block the whole painting in with all the basics of the composition and value. I'll know after the one-minute gesture if I've got it. If I don't, I just get a rag out with some turpentine and wipe it off and do it over again. If I get the gesture of the painting right then the rest of the painting is easy. It's as if the rest of the painting is already done. The color theory I use frees me up for this. All I have to concentrate on is my technique. I don't have to think. I just get to play and have fun. If I play and have fun while painting, it shows up in the final outcome. If I'm struggling with the painting, the angst will show. Whoever is viewing the painting won't be able to explain why but they will sense the struggle. They will be uncomfortable.

I've finished the gesture. Now that the first layer of the complimentary color is done, I will start with the "like" color -- uh oh, what's going on? I pull my headphones off. The noise is almost painful. Two ambulances come flying by. They pull up fifteen feet from where I'm painting. I can't really see anyone behind a pillar to my left. I walk around and on the ground is a lady in her sixties bleeding profusely. The medic is trying to stop the bleeding with wads of bandages. Another medic is trying to get an IV into her. Two more medics whisk her up on a gurney and slide her in the back of the ambulance and off they go with the scream of the siren. I stick my fingers in my ears to lessen the decibels. That poor lady, she was probably on the trip of a lifetime. She probably had planned it for years. Here she is finally retired and with one slip on the cobblestones -- bam. The uneven stones can reap havoc with the simple act of walking. Catch a toe and down you go. The poor woman fell into the corner of the stone base of a column. There she is one minute probably looking around at the wonderful architecture, the people and just taking in the whole scene, and in a flash she's lying on the ground unconscious. Anything can happen when painting plein air. Knowing that she is being taken care of, I put my headphones back on and keep painting.

Our time in Montalcino has been eye opening. We have done trips before; however, nothing like this one. To do a plein-air painting trip for six weeks in one location is indescribable. It is like moving in. There's a big difference with a trip where you are running around from place to place and a trip where you park it in one location and get to know the name of the grocer. One goes back to a favorite restaurant. I look at the menu and I think to myself, "I had that. That was great -- ok, let me try this one."

One night we decide to splurge. We go to the best restaurant in town. It's the middle of the week and we head down. I accidentally fly by the driveway of the restaurant between the stone walls. I then turn around and swing back up the drive and park by the front door. It's a spectacular view overlooking the valley. We walk in and the place is empty. "Table due?" I ask. "No," the hostess replies. Puzzled I ask, "What do you mean? There's no one here." I am told, "When we make a reservation, it is for the evening. All full." Wow. There's no flipping tables here! We made a reservation for later in the week. We then hang around town and enjoy gelato. It also works for dinner!

This being the first plein air-painting trip I've done, I'm quite surprised at how many paintings I've been able to do in such a short amount of time. From the time I wake up in the morning until sunset there is nothing to do but paint, paint, paint.

The panels are all gessoed. There is no lawn to cut, no gallery to tend to, not even mail to open. No distractions. I wake up in the morning and there are only two decisions to make: what size panel do I grab and where do we go for dinner. It's surprising to find out how productive one can be if all you have to do is go out and paint every day. I finish the trip with forty-six finished paintings, although two of them ended up in a dumpster in Tuscany.

We finally make it to the fancy restaurant we made reservations for. We get there and the table is ours for the evening. The meal lasts at least three hours -- I think it was six courses -- everything from soup to nuts. What an unforgettable meal of a lifetime! I can remember ordering our meal from a very charming Italian stud. He looks like he is right out of a really good soap opera. Christine is enjoying the eye candy. She quips, "I know we're married, but I still have eyeballs!" We both laugh out loud.

What an incredible meal -- and I can't forget the expensive wine list -- Brunello de Montalcino, Riserva, Biondi Santi 1957 at six-thousand Euro -- are you kidding me? Wow. We still spent two-hundred fifty Euro for the meal, plus two bottles of wine. The table was ours for the night. It was worth every penny.

A couple of nights later we were wandering through town checking out another restaurant we were interested in. Kiki and I were standing in front of the door and there was a little note taped to it. I had no clue of what it said. My guess is a family wedding, christening, or vacation. We start meandering around in search of another restaurant and lo and behold we run into "Mr. Eye Candy," the waiter from the fancy restaurant. His English is quite good. "What restaurant would you recommend that's not for tourists but one that only the locals go?" He thinks. He looks around and thinks some more. "Come with me, my friends, to the bar. We watch football."

We follow him down a couple of streets to Belvedere Bar. Here Christine and I find ourselves hanging out with real Italians. We are at a local bar with local Italians -- no tourists -- unless we look in the mirror! We're hanging out and having a blast. Alessandro Capitoni, the owner of the bar whose English is quite good, he is our translator. Here we are enjoying the company with about forty Italians, none of which speaks English except our waiter and the owner. It's a small, crummy TV stuck in the corner of the room high in the ceiling as if in a hospital room. It's perfect. I'm not even sure who was playing. I know it's the home team and -- whomever. A commercial then comes on. Christine gets all excited because she knows the Italian soccer player from the TV commercial. "Vodafone" as she points to the TV, "Vodafone, Vodafone." The Italians cheer in jubilant excitement over the fact that she loves their number one player. Life is good!

The meal comes. They offer a prix fixe for an evening of football. Three courses arrive along with fresh baked bread. Alessandro comes around the table with local wine in a big glass jug. He fills everyone's glass. Everyone is relaxing and enjoying the game. It's funny, there are a couple of older Italian men who become fast friends even though we can't communicate one word. They speak the local dialect -- a little different from the official language. It doesn't matter. We're all having a grand time. Most importantly, our Italian friends win the soccer game. They go nuts -- I mean really nuts. They must be a little crazy!

The owner, Alessandro, tells them that we will be in Montalcino for five more weeks. They're all excited. We must come back for Thursday's game. Of course, we agree. The Italians search for any reason to win a game. Alessandro explains that they have chosen us as their unofficial "good luck charm" to win the Cup. God help us. We arrive Thursday and the Italian team is playing the

Americans. This is a little awkward!

Before the game starts, I explain to Alessandro that I have no clue of the names of the players on the U.S. team. The puzzlement in his face says it all. Christine knows the Vodafone guy on the Italian team, but we have no idea of any of the U.S. players. The game is about to start. The Italian national anthem begins. They sing like crazy. It's the U.S. national anthem's turn. Christine and I stand up and put our right hands over our hearts. The Italians were very respectful and clapped vigorously.

The game starts. The Italians know all the subtleties of the game of which I have no clue. I played soccer as a youngster. I was the sweeper. If you know football, you know what that means. We had our meal, our wine and enjoy the game. No one has yet to score. No one scoring is quite an exciting game for the Italians.

And then it happens. The Americans are moving vigorously towards the Italian goal trying to get the elusive ball into the net. In the blink of an eye, an American, with fervor, slams the ball towards the prized goal. The ball then ricochets off one of the Italian players and squeaks in -- score! The U.S. takes the lead. They freak out. I stand up and bow to them politely, thanking them for the assistance with the goal. The look on their faces -- priceless!

The game ends up as a tie. "You must come to the next game," Alessandro insists, being that we are their "good luck charm." Feeling obliged to accommodate our new friends, we promise to return for Friday's game.

In total, we see four Cup matches. The Italian team wins three with one tie against the Americans. They keep advancing and we have a whole new group of friends. A number of the older gentlemen are friends by handshake, facial expressions and gesture only. Our English and their Italian don't exactly meet in the middle -- it doesn't matter. We have the game, food and wine. All is good.

We arrive at our last game. It's a beautiful evening and Alessandro has set up the meal outside in front of his bar. We always ate inside during the previous games. However, it is a late game tonight so I guess we are all going to have our prix fixe beforehand. What a nice evening to be sitting outside. The weather is terrific. After the meal is cleared from the tables, three ladies from Canada join Christine and I.

The Italians have congregated around the TV prior to the game discussing what is about to happen. We talk with the Canadians about their journey. They were first in Paris for a week before coming to Tuscany for week number two. They quite enjoyed Paris. However, on more than one occasion the Parisians really ticked them off. Here they are French speaking Canadians and the Parisians would pretend that they couldn't understand a word they were saying. How rude. They have an accent and because their French isn't exactly how the Parisians talk, they would ignore them and pretend that they didn't understand a word they said. After a couple glasses of wine, the ladies exclaim, "Fuck the French! We love Italy." Alessandro retrieves us -- the game is about to start -- and invites the Canadians to join in. One Canadian comments, "The French would never have asked us to join in on their party. This is awesome!"

The Italians are nervous. This is a big game. If they win this, they are in the finals. Their national anthem starts. Everyone sings their hearts out as loud as they can. One can hear it reverberate from all over town! I must say that I've never really appreciated a national anthem one can sing to. "America the Beautiful" looks really good right now.

The game is tied in overtime, which leads to a second overtime -- a tripping penalty by the other team. Our friends go nuts. Now I'm starting to understand the rules of a penalty kick. I believe that since the tripping was inside the goalie's box, there are no blockers on the penalty kick. It is just between the one tripped and the goalie. Score! It's over.

Just like that, they move into the finals. Our new friends celebrate with great enthusiasm, but there's a problem. Alessandro makes an announcement in Italian. The looks on their faces turn to great concern. Alessandro explains to us about "the ball." Just like in the game with the Americans "the ball" was deflected off an Italian player for an American score. Anything can happen in this sport. It's like another person on the field. Anyone has a chance of winning because of "the ball."

"You have become our good luck charm over the past four matches to help us with the ball. Now that you are leaving, we have a problem." Alessandro continues. "However, I think I may have a remedy." He announces to all that they will transfer the "good luck" from the Americans to the Canadians -- both speak English, the same continent -- good enough! They all cheer in excitement.

The next thing I know, everyone has gathered outside. One fellow who speaks no English has a little yellow MG sports car. I guess it's from the late 50's or early 60's. Alessandro then explains the process of transferring the luck from the Americans to the Canadians via the flag. We then happily climb on board the MG sitting on the trunk with our feet jammed into the tiny space behind the seats and off we go. He takes off like a bat out of hell. I almost lose the flag. It takes the both of us to hold onto it. He is whizzing through town around the sharp corners and honking his horn like a crazy fool! The whole town is celebrating in the streets. Everyone in town is hooting and hollering as we pass. We barely hold on. We make the final turn to the front of the bar. Everyone is rejoicing in the successful transfer of the luck. All is good! We can all sleep well tonight. Christine and I say our long goodbyes to everyone. This was our third trip through Montalcino. We promise to return again someday. Ciao.

3 EXHIBITION IN FRANCE

I've had a number of exhibitions in the Leleu Gallery in Doylestown, Pennsylvania -- not solo shows, but group shows. They sold fairly well. That is to say, nothing great, nothing bad. One evening I swung by an opening that Frederic and Lisa Leleu were having for a couple of artists I respected. I was roaming around the gallery. It was the usual good crowd. It seemed like they were selling fairly well. Lisa, who is quite the beautiful lady with huge eyes and long dark hair, walks up to me and with no hesitation asks, "Would you like to have an exhibition in France?" "Of course," I reply with enthusiasm. Sometimes it's just that simple. Lisa and Frederic knew my work quite well -- not just from the shows at their gallery, but from visits they made to my gallery in Lambertville. I remember one artist I know who said to me, "Wow, you're lucky to have an exhibition in France." It really ticked me off. The thing is "luck" had nothing to do with it. I've had a number of shows with the Leleu's, had numerous sales and commissions done through their gallery. The Leleu's could tell how well it's been going at my own gallery. They know that I have the wherewithal to handle my responsibilities and successfully pull off an exhibition in Frederic's hometown in Laon, France. No such thing as "luck." Preparation equals opportunity -- that's one of my favorite sayings. The Leleu's really wanted this to work out well. Their brainstorm was to have an artists' exchange. They would send American artists to a gallery in Laon, France and the gallery owner there would send French artists to their gallery in the United States. They chose me to be their first American for the exchange of artists. This was quite a compliment, considering they deal with about twenty-five artists in their gallery and are friends with many more.

I brought twenty-two paintings for the exhibit of local scenes, figurative work and even a few paintings from the Grand

Canyon and Bryce Canyon for variety. I then checked into all the methods of shipping, USPS, UPS, FedEx, et cetera, -- ridiculous! This is not just the cost factor, but also the time frame.

By freighter, it takes six weeks and they don't even guarantee that time frame. By air and with the weight of the framed paintings -- which arm do you want? This was too cost prohibitive. I decided to pack the paintings in our luggage. Christine and I can bring four bags on the plane at eighty pounds each, plus two carry-ons. We have a total of three-hundred twenty pounds for the artwork and our travel stuff. One bag with the largest paintings is oversized. I'll get charged eighty bucks for going over the size limit. That will work! The other three bags are no problem. The smaller paintings are packed in and around clothing for cushioning.

We finally get to the airport. It's a struggle with all the weight of the bags. They came in at about seventy-five pounds each. Customs goes smoothly and we're off. Wow. I can't believe it. My first solo exhibition overseas at the age of thirty-six and it's still sinking in. We land in Paris. All is good. We're waiting for the luggage -- still waiting for the luggage. We wait -- now I'm beginning to get worried. Finally they come. I can see that the luggage is in ruins. They were opened up by customs with luggage straps eschew. I can see damaged paintings. I sigh. There's nothing I can do. I wrap them up and tie the luggage straps the best I can. I load them onto one of the luggage carts and we're off -- whoa, not so fast. While I was putting everything back together, apparently a group of customs officials were watching the whole thing. They wanted to know what all the paintings were about. I had had French from third until the sixth grade and not a lick since. In anticipation of a problem, I pulled out of my coat pocket the French press release for the show and the exhibition mailer.

The customs officials then pass the information around between themselves nodding their heads up and down. I couldn't understand a word they were saying. However, I could tell they were amused and a bit impressed that here was this American coming to France having an exhibition of his impressionistic work. I think they took it as kind of a compliment.

We get the car -- no problem there, it all fits in the Fiat --

barely, but it fits. It's about ten-thirty in the morning and we're off -- tired but feeling great. We have about a three-hour drive ahead. There should be no commuter traffic to run into. We go north from the Charles de Gaulle Airport on a major highway towards the center of Paris. Route Two goes northeast a straight shot up to Laon for the exhibit. We're ten minutes out and there's my exit. I spotted it just up ahead. It's a little weird driving for the first time with all the signs in another language -- oh no, the highway divided with an express lane and a local lane. Here I am stuck in the express lane with a truck blocking my move towards the exit. Ok, now I'm clear -- uh-oh, now of all things a Jersey barrier blocking me. Shit! There goes my exit.

Well, it's still early. It took us at least an hour to get back on track on Route Two -- not easy after a long flight! I hope that the rest of the trip goes a little smoother.

We arrive in Laon late in the afternoon. We drive into the hilltop town and being lost, Christine makes me ask someone for directions. If I weren't so tired I would never have asked. I pull out the mailer for the exhibit and point to the address on the card with a confused look on my face. This nice man tries to explain where to go. I think he's trying to tell me about one-way streets. He then gives up. Obviously, he can tell I'm not getting it. He directs me to follow him.

We then follow him through a maze of tiny streets that eventually open up to a plaza and then down a one-way alley to the other side of town. He stops in front of the gallery. He points, waves and off he goes. It was really nice of him to help us out. It would have taken me at least an hour to find this place on my own.

We meet up with the gallery owners, Hervé and his wife. I think my terrible French is better than his almost nonexistent English. We somehow manage between our English/French, French/English dictionaries. He proceeds to take us a few blocks away to Frederic's parents' house -- that's the connection to this town. Frederic Leleu grew up here. We knew from Frederic that his parents were on vacation in Spain. They had generously invited us to stay at their cottage in the back courtyard of their house.

We arrive in front of a high wall with a door in it. He opens it up to a wonderful hidden garden. There are beautiful plantings with all the pleasures of outdoor living. He then leads us to the cottage. It has two floors, small but quaint, with a little balcony off the bedroom. We have it all to ourselves.

It's now about eight o'clock in the evening. The sun is going down. We are going to sleep like a couple of logs tonight! We agreed to meet with Hervé to begin setting up the exhibition at noon tomorrow after a good night's sleep.

We wake up at about eight o'clock. The birds are chirping. Low and behold, a coffee maker! This is going to taste so good. I make the Joe and we hang out on the veranda overlooking the gardens. The morning dew is everywhere with ivy all along the iron railings. There is a chill in the air. It's the middle of June, I thought it would be a bit warmer. Christine grabs a sweater. She gets chilled easily. I'm the opposite. It feels great.

We venture out through the door to the outside world on the other side of the wall. We meander down the extremely narrow streets. Some of the streets are so narrow that the old Mini Coopers barely make it through. The sidewalks have just enough room to stand sideways all the while leaving you pinned against the buildings

47

as the cars go whizzing by.

We get to the gallery. It hasn't opened yet. We excitedly peek into the large space. it has high ceilings. What a beautiful space for a show in what looks like a good location right off the main plaza. It's time to find a café for a cappuccino and a bite to eat. We both seem to be recovering fairly well from the time change -- a little sleepy eyed, but ok. We have a little time before meeting with Hervé . We then walk around the perimeter wall of this quaint town and get to see the vistas of the area for the first time. There are layers upon layers of fields going into the horizon as far as one's eye can see. You are greeted with green fields, green fields and more green fields. The views into the distance from the vantage point on the hill are just magical.

After our jaunt, we hop into the Fiat and head down to the gallery with the paintings to unload. Hervé greets us and helps us unload all the paintings into the gallery. Christine and I will be in France for two weeks. We have allotted five days for the exhibit and the rest of the time to cruise around to see all that we can. After the exhibit, Hervé will then ship the balance of what doesn't sell back to the States.

We spend a day or so setting up the exhibition. I brought just the right amount of paintings, twenty three. This is a fascinating building for an exhibition. Its history goes back to the thirteenth century. Various parts of the four-story building were built over six centuries. The floor alone had wood, tile, concrete, stone and what other materials, I don't even know. The walls varied in materials also, very eclectic. It even had different levels with a balcony and extremely high ceilings. The front was all modern glass from floor to ceiling with great visibility of the artwork by all on the street.

We now have some time for day trips before the show. Anything Hervé needs now we can accomplish at night. Christine and I head out for Reims. I want to see the Cathedral. Looking at the map, it looks like a nice drive into the country. We plan to stop by a small town or two along the way just to check it out and have a cappuccino. We make it to Reims by noontime with my camera in tow.

I have been taking pictures like mad. I have enough film for about twelve-hundred photos, twenty-four rolls of film with two lead lined bags so the x-ray machines on the flight home don't ruin them. It's normally only the high ASA film you have to worry about getting destroyed by x-ray. After walking around a while, we do a little window-shopping and pick up a set of four crystal wine glasses. At the moment, we only have coffee mugs back at the cottage to have some nice local wine in -- this just will not do! This is our first memento to bring home to enjoy as a remembrance of the trip. We sit in a café and say yes to another cappuccino. The size of the cups are much smaller than home. You're not going to find a twenty-ounce here, let alone a twelve-ounce. The cappuccinos are small and cheap. The franc to dollar ratio is about seven to one. Last night we had a three-course prix fixe meal with two bottles of local wine over three hours at a very cute little restaurant in Laon for the equivalence of fourteen U.S. dollars -- very nice, indeed.

Here we sit at a café in Reims, almost in the same position that Monet painted the cathedral all those many times. I point out to Christine the window where Monet must have rented the space the summer he wasn't feeling well. He painted the cathedral on the same size canvas with the same composition many, many times, just changing the color theories he was using. Every day the lighting was different from morning, afternoon and dusk, all the while creating a new painting each time.

The following day, we head up towards the Belgium border. It looks like fairly untraveled country, as far as tourists go. It ends up being my favorite part of the trip as far as the landscape goes with beautiful rolling hills and farms that have been untouched for centuries. We got quite a number of unusual looks as we went through a couple of tiny, tiny towns with the quizzical expression, "They must be lost. There's nothing here for tourists!"

When traveling, I am the driver because Kiki doesn't like to drive in strange places. She's designated the map-reader. This leaves me in total control of stopping to take pictures whenever I like. I must have been driving Christine crazy -- we stop a lot. Sometimes we will be driving down a road with great landscapes on each side. I'll even take photographs while the car is moving.

The scheduled time for the exhibition is six o'clock. Everything is set. Christine looks fabulous in a sleek, black dress. The athlete she is, she blows away any perception the French may have of the out-of-shape American. The crowd starts arriving.

Some are obviously good friends of Hervé and his wife, while others seem to be clients who are scoping out the art. With an opening, you can count on a few locals getting a free meal with hors d'oeuvres and wine. People are the same no matter where you go. I constantly see the same mix of people at the openings in the Lambertville / New Hope area. We also get the serious customers and those who are there only for the food. I chuckle to myself.

This opening is a little strange for me. There are only two people here that I can communicate with. There is one lady who I think came just so she could practice her English. The other one turns out to be an interpreter. Hervé informs me that I am to give a speech -- well, nothing like short notice! The gallery now has about seventy-five people in it. A photographer from a newspaper arrives. The interpreter speaks. I can pick out a few words here and there -- "American," "painter," "impressionist," "New York," "Frederic Leleu."

Still speaking in French, the interpreter makes an obvious introduction of Hervé as the gallery owner along with his wife. He then introduces me with a gesture to start my speech. I just wing it.

Let's start with pleasantries. "Thank you, Hervé. Thank you Frederic and Lisa Leleu for giving me the opportunity to exhibit my work in France. What a wonderful time my wife and I are having exploring your part of this wonderful country. Everyone has been so nice to us during our travel."

I then proceed to explain the details of how I work, from my color theory, studio work versus plein air, the initial gesture of the painting all the way down to the final protective varnish used. I think I did a pretty good job of just winging it.

In the blink of an eye, the opening is over. The exhibition continues for another six weeks. We pack up our luggage from the cottage. We now have just our carry on bags. We are now traveling very light. Frederic's parents have returned from Spain. We knock on their front door to the main house. We do the usual pleasantries and I give them a small painting of the Lambertville canal as a gift for staying at their home.

We then jump in the rental car and are now cruising through France. We wing the rest of the trip. We have a general idea of where we want to go; however, no timetables. We head north of

Paris on our way to Giverny, then down to the Loire Valley and finish up in Paris for a few days.

We make our way to Giverny after spending two days photographing the countryside in small towns north of Paris. We simply cruise in the general direction of where we want to go. "Look over there, that looks neat. Let's check it out," and off we go to explore.

We arrive in Giverny early in the morning just as they open. We wander into the gardens in front of Monet's house. It's the end of June, the perfect time for everything to be in spectacular bloom. All the colors are just exploding. The paths between the flowering rows are tight to walk through. Everything is in full growth. What a great place Monet built where he could just walk out his front door and paint his heart out.

We walk inside Monet's house. It looks just as one would expect. We wander through the various rooms down the hallway into his bedroom. There's great light in the bedroom with large windows overlooking the gardens. It's quite a large room for an old stone house. I then start to notice all the Japanese prints on the walls. I had read in various history books of the fascination the French Impressionists had with the art of Japanese wood block prints. I became very familiar with them at RISD and had even collected and studied them myself. My eye spots Utamaro; that's the cream of the crop in collecting these prints. He is the best of the best. I see another Utamaro and a couple of names that I'm not familiar with, then even more Utamaro. Wow! There's more than twenty of them with no guards or anyone around keeping them safe. I check out one of them. Holy cow, it's not even secured to the wall. It's just as it would have been when Monet was there.

We then go into his studio. The studio is huge. You could even drop a basketball court in there and have plenty of room left over. It's all steel beam construction. That makes sense to me. How long after the Eiffel tower was it built? I'm sure he built it for those huge paintings of the lily pads he did for the MET in New York City and all the other museums. One could certainly tell that he was doing extremely well financially.

We then work our way over to the lily ponds. They even put a tunnel under the road for the tourists to get across the street to the ponds. This must have been for safety reasons, I'm sure. By this time, it's afternoon. Busload after busload now arrive from Paris. They are going up to the house first so we have the ponds almost to ourselves.

My camera has been working overtime -- snap, snap, snap. I then change the lens -- snap, snap, snap. I keep shooting like crazy, burning through my film. It's magnificent everywhere you look. We spend about an hour walking through the paths of the ponds a couple of times. The hoards of tourists from all of the buses start crowding us. It's now time to leave and head to the Loire Valley.

We start our longest drive of the trip down through La Mans to Tours. This is the only place besides Paris that we reserved a hotel. We had just been stopping at places in little towns that intrigued us and would ask if they had a room. We would check out the available rooms. If we liked one, we would take it or just move on. Most of these were mom and pop establishments with usually about six to eight rooms with a café or a restaurant on the first floor. They were somewhat like a small B&B in the States.

After about a seven-hour long drive, we arrive in Tours. The sun is going down. We are both very tired at this point. We pull into the hotel and I'm wondering if we aren't in New Brunswick, New Jersey. There are strip malls all around and the hotel looks very seedy. We are too tired to wander around and try to find something else. It's a room with a bed. At this point, I don't really care. We plan on taking off the first thing in the morning, anyway. We then check in. We are late. They grumble and we get our room. The queen-sized bed barely fits in the room. We are in a cave right on the highway. We look at one another. We'll never do this again. This is the last time we're going to reserve a hotel in advance! The other places were fantastic. Thank God for the air conditioner. I crank it up to drown out the trucks. Now the trucks can't even keep us up. We sleep great, and we're off at five a.m. as fast as we can.

We are now heading across to the Loire Valley going west. We have no idea where we're going. We have about four days until we finish up in Paris. We do what has become a ritual of stopping at a small town that looks interesting for our morning cappuccino and a bite to eat. Christine has taken a liking to the figs in France. There are many shops that have a variety of goods such as cheese, fruit, veggies, smoked meats hanging from the ceiling, fresh baked breads

-- and, of course, figs on a string. There are usually about a dozen dried figs tied together. Kiki loves to get these. She likes to keep them in her pocketbook. Periodically she pulls a fig off the string and -- its snack time! This is a little piece of heaven for her.

We're back in the car and off we go. I make a point to stay off the highways. I like the secondary roads for exploring so we don't accidentally bypass something of interest -- uh-oh, we're now stuck. How can we have a traffic jam? I then see the funny uniforms of the French police with the pointy hats. They have the streets blocked off and there's nowhere to go. I can't figure out what is going on. They don't really seam to be directing anyone around the blocked road. We're stuck just sitting. A bit of time goes by. My turn to have one of the figs -- quite good!

I now see a serious bicyclist. He looks like a real pro with his bright colored garb whizzing by. The police make us wait, and wait some more. I then note all these intense colors in the distance coming towards us. The landscape is flat as a board here, so you can see quite far. The intense colors are now coming even closer to us. It's best described as a swarm -- yes, a swarm of bees chasing something down, working like a team to hunt down the single one in front. I'd say there were two-hundred in the swarm. It's hard to tell when it's all a blur. I see now that this portion of a bicycle race is over. The policeman then removes the orange cones in the street and off we go.

Exploring with no set agenda is such fun. There is a sense of freedom when you have no rigid time line to follow. As we roam down the Loire River, in the distance, we see an interesting looking town. The architecture of the main bridge is fabulous. We cross. Half way across the bridge, I spot a hotel. You can tell from the distance it's a mom and pop B&B, our kind of place. There is a plaza in front with parking. We pull up and there is a café on the first floor. It looks great. We inquire about the price of a room. My French is awful and the lady of the house's English is just as bad. Somehow we communicate just fine. She escorts us up to the third floor to a corner room facing the bridge and the plaza. The room has two small balconies with light beaming in the huge windows. She politely excuses herself so that we can make our decision. There's only one decision to make here. We were only planning to stay here for one night. I proceed downstairs to inquire if three nights are possible. She replies, "Oui, oui." After calculating the exchange rate it came to $45 a night. You can't beat that!

We then dump our stuff from the car, quickly freshen up and off we go to wander the streets and see what's around. Yes, another cappuccino is in order. We eventually make it back to our place late in the afternoon with a bottle of local wine and some cheese we picked up at one of the shops. Christine takes a nap and I sit on the balcony with wine in one of our new crystal glasses and a chunk of cheese whose name I don't have a prayer of pronouncing. I cut slices off with my pocketknife -- fantastique.

The river is in front of me. The bridge, with its shimmering evening lights, start to pop on with the violet hues of dusk settling in. It feels really good knowing we're going to be here for a stretch of time. We were in Laon for only a few days. However, between the exhibition, day trips and our own excitement, we've been on the run the whole time. It's time to relax.

The wine and cheese at this moment in time tastes spectacular. I'd just had my first exhibition in France and am now touring around the countryside. It doesn't get much better than this.

I hadn't even noticed the series of trucks that had gathered below me in the plaza. There were a number of men scurrying around moving all kinds of things. Some had carts, some with stuff over their shoulders, some carrying some sort of equipment -- scaffolding perhaps? I keep enjoying my wine and cheese. This is my dinner, wine and cheese. A stage is being set up. This is interesting. I wonder what is going on. I decide to stretch my legs and venture out to get a better look at the goings-on. I head down the stairs through the café onto the plaza and witness a grand operation in progress. I stroll through the plaza, and in one truck I can see them starting to unload large amplification systems. With the size of them, I don't think it's going to be a play -- maybe music?

As I head back up to my room, I see in the window of the café a poster for an international music festival. The dates are for today, tomorrow and the next -- what luck! I scurry up the uneven, ancient steps to our room to tell Kiki of the wonderful surprise. That night we relax at our balcony overlooking the plaza listening to bands from all around the world.

The next few days are filled roaming around the countryside

taking pictures for future paintings. We come home in the afternoon walking the streets to discover musical groups in all the plazas, fountain areas and churches. We come across group after group. They vary in size ranging from a simple soloist to large ensembles. What a find these few days are.

Paris, the last stop on our sojourn. We have a hotel reserved on the outskirts. This is the only one I could find on the web for a reasonable price. The World Cup is in France this year being played at the same time as our trip. Before we left, I was told to forget it. At this date, you won't find a thing in Paris. After our debacle in Tours, I decide that we should drive to the center of town and drop the car off at the Esplanade des Invalides. We then hoof it with our luggage in tow. We drag our stuff along the Seine a couple of blocks towards Notre Dame. I come across a posh hotel, hoping they can at least send me in the right direction. To my surprise, they have a room and it's affordable. Actually, it's cheaper than the one I reserved on the outskirts of town. I head out to the street to fetch Kiki. She's checking out the scene, not expecting something right away. "I found us a room!" With surprise in her eyes, I grab her bag, head to the lobby and we're escorted to a beautiful room. This was almost too easy.

It's eleven in the morning, and we have the whole day ahead of us. We walk the streets of Paris and, of course, get a cappuccino in a café. We stop in a quaint little shop featuring all the wonderful foods you can imagine in Europe: fresh vegetables, dried fruits, smoked meats, all kinds of cheeses and things to delight one's palette. One thing is for sure, you will not be seeing any Styrofoam or Saran Wrap. We get the standard baguette, some cheese, grapes and olives -- what a culinary treat. We then stroll across the Siene to the gardens outside the Lourve where we enjoy a lovely picnic.

Tomorrow's plan is to go to the Musée d'Orsay -- or lovingly referred to as, "The train station museum." This is the museum in Paris that I am most interested in. The impressionist collection is possibly the best in the world. When we arrive, we are delighted at only a few minutes' wait. What an incredible space for exhibiting beautiful paintings. Breathtaking. Musée d'Orsay is big and open with natural light streaming in and filling every landscape. Plein air, in the open with natural light.

I'm interested in another museum with an exhibit of

Velasquez. We get to the front door. It's closed. I'm very disappointed -- closed on Tuesdays. I hadn't noticed this in the tourist info that we had gathered before the trip. The first screw up so far -- well, I never said I was perfect! That's all the museums we will make an effort to see.

When I was a kid, my mother had taken me to the Met hundreds of times. What can I say, I'm far more interested in the process of finding scenes to paint than going to museums. Most people would think this is sacrilegious for a painter. I'm a painter not an art historian. My main focus is on creating art, not studying other people's art.

Our trip is winding down. We have had wonderful experiences. When I started drawing and painting as a kid, I never pictured I would be having an exhibit in France and cruising through Europe. I just loved to draw and paint. Now here I am as an adult being paid to do what I love -- marveilleux.

4 HOME SWEET HOME

For about two months, I've been working in the studio on paintings from the trip to France of poppy fields and landscapes fading into the horizon and just having fun. That's part of my philosophy, you must have fun when you're painting. If you are struggling with the work, the struggle will be evident in the painting. Any person viewing the painting will sense the struggle. They won't be able to put their finger on it or tell you why the painting doesn't work for them. They will sense the difficulty you had in doing the painting.

Conversely, if you are having a grand time playing with the paint and really enjoying the process, that joy will come out in the finished piece. It has to. There is nothing you can do about it.

The first couple of paintings are finished. I hang them in my gallery without expectation. I figured there was no down side. I had had a great exhibition, I traveled through France and had a great time. And here we are. Great fun. If nothing else, maybe I will be able to command a higher price with my regular paintings of the local area. Let's say a doctor comes into the gallery looking to buy a painting. "Oh, I see you've had a solo exhibition in France." He will now be able to justify, in his mind, a price he might have otherwise balked at.

I sold two paintings of France right away -- nice! That was awesome. I scrounge through photos to decide what to paint next. It's fun reliving all the memories and getting paid for it at the same time. I decide on the next round of paintings and get to work. I then decide to mix it up: a château here, a café there and a vista everywhere. I paint my little heart out. I keep painting them and I keep selling them over and over. It's not that I hadn't been selling my regular local work. After all, I've had my own gallery exclusively showing my own work for five years now. The work shown at my gallery is typically paintings of the area, the Delaware River, the canals, Lambertville, New Hope and the farms in the surrounding area.

I then have a light bulb moment -- I get these once in a while. The people who can afford to travel to wonderful places can also afford to buy oil paintings. Let's say they travel to Paris and Giverny and spend a lot of money on the trip. As a result, they will want mementos to bring home. Large oil paintings are difficult to bring home on an airplane. Consequently, you have to ship it. "How much extra is that going to cost? What about insuring it during shipment, will it even arrive? What will my recourse be if my painting never arrives? Oh, forget it. It's too much of a hassle." They come into my gallery some time after, say, their honeymoon in Paris. "Look, honey, a painting of the Seine in Paris! Do you remember our walks in the evening after dinner with the sun going down and the boats on the river? Ah, those were wonderful memories." After consideration, "How much is that painting? We'll take it!"

I like to call it "association." People may love a piece of art for the painting itself. However, all that stuff they teach you in art school: composition, value, color, line, shape, negative shape, texture, brush work, warm, cool, perspective, scale, movement will only get you ninety-five percent of the way to selling your artwork.

People will not pull out their wallet or purse and happily hand you their hard earned money with a smile on their face and a big thank you without having an association or memory with the piece of art.

That elusive five percent is the difference between starving and selling so much work that you can't keep up.

We live in a beautiful tourist town. We are an eclectic community of artists, writers, poets, sculptors, dancers, musicians and the like. People travel from New York, Philadelphia and from around the world to our charming town of Lambertville. This is a great place to get away from one's far too busy life and sit back and relax for a few days. People can go tubing or canoeing on the Delaware River, enjoy a bike ride on the canal path, visit the many antique shops and galleries or enjoy a great meal at one of the various ethnic restaurants. Visitors might sit out at one of the numerous cafés just like in Europe.

Visitors often stay at one of the many B&B's in the area. There are seventy-four B&B's on my mailing list and that only covers about a ten-mile radius. We are really blessed to live in such a wonderful area. When Christine and I came back from this trip, we were walking on the canal a day or so later and it struck us that this area is just as beautiful as the great places we had just traveled to. It has given me a whole new appreciation and new perspective for painting in the area I live. I now see Bucks and Hunterdon Counties in a whole new "light."

After enjoying their time in the area, tourists and locals stroll to my gallery on Bridge Street in Lambertville to see paintings of the memories they just created. The five percent is already there. I have, I hope, already done the other ninety-five percent. The painting has to be an excellent piece of artwork. If it's mediocre, it doesn't matter if they have the association, they aren't going to spend money on an inferior piece of art. If you want to sell your paintings, you have to have the ninety-five percent and the five percent together.

You also can't hide in your studio. You have to get your artwork out there anyway you can. I often get artists in my gallery asking me various questions. I will ask them, "How many paintings do you have in your studio?" The answer is typically thirty or forty. I tell them they aren't doing their job. I always get the same baffled look on their faces. "What do you mean?" I will reply, "Your paintings should be in galleries, juried shows, alternative shows, in restaurants and the like. How is anyone going to see your work if you are hiding them in your studio? How is anyone going to buy your work if it's not seen?" Then I get the usual response, "Oh, I never thought about it that way before."

The third piece of the puzzle is location, location, location, just like in real estate. If you desire to sell your artwork, you have to have all three of these lined up: the ninety-five percent, the five percent, and location. For example, a friend of mine does fantastic work painting, sculptures and ceramics -- all excellent quality. He has the ninety-five percent. He and his wife have a gallery in Lambertville. They have the location. He can't sell his work because he is missing the five percent. No association. He will never be able to sell his work here in Lambertville. The reason for this is that his style runs along the lines of Picasso's later work. His work is fabulous. He is originally from Portugal. He needs to be in a great tourist town in Portugal or Spain with his own gallery. The association. The tourists will have the association with their great trip and Miguel's Picasso-esce work. Consequently, he would have a difficult time keeping up with demand.

I have always loved doing landscape paintings. That's why I live and work in this area. If I loved to do cityscapes, I would live and work in New York. An artist friend of mine who does Southwest art, he lives in Sedona. In other words, I'm not going to try to sell my local Bucks County scenes in Miami, Florida! That would be like trying to sell a fur coat in Hawaii or selling skimpy bathing suits in Gnome, Alaska. You might sell a few but -- good luck, that's fighting an uphill battle. It's far easier coasting downhill than fighting gravity in an uphill climb.

5 PROVENCE

I'm sitting at my easel painting away in the back of my gallery one day. This fellow comes in and introduces himself as Harry Jackendorff. "I was walking by your gallery and saw a painting of Paris in the window." I proceed to tell him about our trip and show him paintings of France I have in the gallery. He is quite interested in the work. He then explains that he recently bought a house in Provence and wants to open a gallery on the first floor of the building.

Harry then asks if I would be interested in staying at his house in Provence to help him set up a gallery. I would work on paintings in the south of France to sell to the tourist trade and basically help him with getting the gallery off the ground. We meet a couple of times to set in concrete the details of our new adventure.

Off we go for a two-week trip through Provence. I then think to myself how this is feeding on itself. First there was my exhibition in France. As a result, this fellow sees my work; consequently, a trip to Provence. Maybe this is something I can capitalize on. This is what I call a "run around trip." We plan to spend a few days in the town of Contignac at Harry's house. Harry and I had come to the conclusion that paintings and prints from other parts of Provence besides Contignac would sell well at the gallery. Tourists who visit Contignac probably have been through St. Tropez, Arles and Saint-Paul-de-Provence. Contignac isn't a huge destination point, and to have the other more popular destinations in the repertoire would be a good idea. We also pondered about wholesaling prints to galleries in other towns such as St. Tropez for another source of income.

We are headed to Provence. Weeks are spent in my easy chair mulling through travel books and reviewing possible destinations -- not day to day, but rather highlights with a basic travel route. We will fly into Niece. Then there's the usual rush at the airport. We'll grab the car and off we go. We head up to Saint-Paul-de-Provence in the hills above Niece. We are, of course, very excited about roaming around for the next two weeks.

Saint-Paul, the road north into the mountains of what you might call the "mini canyons of the southwest." We then make our way towards Contignac. On our route, we pass through Draguignan, a tiny scrap of a town with one little street. We park. We're hungry. Looking for a place to eat, we pass an old inn with white tablecloths. We just want something quick and simple. We're tired. We walk down the street searching for something to eat. It's now about eight o'clock. Finally, a place that looks open. Pizza, oh well, we're hungry. This will have to do. Obviously, there's no other place in town. We take a seat in the back of the open restaurant. This will help shelter Christine from any breeze because it's starting to get chilly out. We then order our pizza from the fellow behind the counter in French -- well, sort of. We are working on our French and he is working on his English so we meet in the middle.

He stokes his oven with a few pieces of wood to get the fire up to temperature. We order the local wine and we begin a wonderful conversation -- small talk at first, then as we get more comfortable, we move into a variety of topics. We are his only customers for the evening so we are talkative. Christine explains that I'm an artist and there's instant camaraderie. He asks many questions, such as where we live in the States and what brings us to Draguignan and so on. The pizza arrives at our table. It's fabulous with a thin crust and topped with fresh ingredients, great spices, olive oil and some Romano cheese he grinds on top. It was perfect. It was so relaxing. We took our time and chilled out. We didn't want to leave. However, it's time to move onto our destination for the next few days in Contignac. It takes us about half an hour from our pizza joint to Harry's house. We arrive in the dark. Thankfully, Harry had drawn a map for us outlining the parking and the location of the house. It's about ten o'clock in the evening and time to get settled in, brush our teeth and crash.

It's the morning and I'm up fairly early. Christine is still sleeping. I wander out into the quaint village. I stretch my legs while walking across the cobblestones. It's very quiet and peaceful.

I work my way back to Harry's house and climb the front steps overlooking the plaza. The ancient church next door is the main attraction for tourists visiting the timeless town of Contignac. It's now time to make the java. This has become my job when traveling. When home in Lambertville, Kiki always makes breakfast and java. I don't know how this tradition started, it just did, and I like it!

It's a simple house, wonderful in its simplicity. The house is a total of five stories, one room per floor all stacked one upon another. The basement level comprises the town's fish store. My understanding from Harry is that it's open a scant two days a week. In addition, the owner services two fish stores in adjoining towns. The first floor is a generous living room and kitchen with a spiral staircase upstairs to a bedroom and large bathroom. You travel further up the stairs to another bedroom. At the top, you reach the attic space Harry envisions to renovate.

We have our morning coffee. They have a coffee press here. I think presses make the best coffee. It tastes fantastic. We then wander the streets exploring our new destination and playground.

It's a quaint town situated in a valley with small shops, a few restaurants, a bar and a café. The main plaza has a hardware store, a bakery and the town's only high-end restaurant. After a second cup of coffee, I stand at Harry's front porch and ponder how this could work as a gallery.

The front of the house looks over the plaza -- not the main plaza, but just adjacent to it. The front of the house can easily accommodate all kinds of art: paintings, prints and note cards. Finally, there is display space available on the sidewalk. This would work very well towards drawing people into the gallery.

Over the next couple of days, we wander through the local area photographing and hiking. Contignac is a very picturesque area. I'm envisioning many paintings. It's quiet and peaceful in Contignac. While photographing, we travel to Les Salles, St. Tropez, Aups, Salernes and many more small towns. We love the small towns. That must be why we love our town of Lambertville!

We have enjoyed hanging around Contignac the last few days. We basically moved in. Ah, this is a beautiful way to travel. You have the luxury of staying put and intimately befriending the locals. You have the joy of your day-to-day shopping at the local market while having espresso and discussing the days' news. Our time here is unfortunately ending. However, we plan to return to Contignac at the end of our trip.

Now we start the run around part of the trip. We head west. As you know, this is how we tend to travel, just winging it. We have no hotel reservations, no timetable. We are just wandering. We have a general idea of where we want to go and that's it.

Aix-en-Provence. We arrive early in the morning. Back in Contignac, Christine's hairdryer just didn't like the 220 volts. She yells, "What's wrong with this thing?" I run over and the hairdryer is in flames with an intense, glowing orange ball about to catch Harry's house on fire! I yank the plug and put the now melting plastic smoking glob on the stone patio outside. Disaster averted.

We now find ourselves at the Aix-en Provence Monoprix. It's a department store, very nice. Kiki is finally going to get a Euro hairdryer we can bring on future trips and not cause a fire. I'm hanging outside photographing the cafés and people watching. I hear this screaming, "Gordon, Gordon!" I run back to the entrance of the Monoprix and Christine is beside herself. "My wallet, my wallet, I've lost my wallet." While she was shopping, she put it down somewhere in the department store. Thinking to myself, where do I start, I speak to the ladies at the counter. After a few minutes they understand what I'm talking about, lost and found. Maybe my third grade French actually sunk in. "No," it hasn't been turned in, I'm told.

We try to backtrack Christine's steps in the store, here there and everywhere. This is a nightmare! Her credit cards and the money she put aside for spending on the trip, all gone. One of the ladies at the counter calls me over. Someone has turned in a wallet. Lucky me. I open it and all the contents are there, cash and everything. What a good feeling that someone did the right thing. A lost wallet is quite an annoyance. You have the phone calls to credit card companies, replacing your driver's license and insurance card -- yes, a real pain. For Christine, possibly losing her wallet was a monumental happening. We are relieved. Life is good.

St Remy. Christine discovered an interesting place in one of our travel books. She is very good at utilizing information offering places to stay, restaurants, places of interest and historical landmarks. Chateau de Roussan gave intriguing details to peak our interest. "Visit for its character and setting, but not if you expect sanitized luxury. The ancient farmhouse on the grounds once belonged to Nostradamus." On the map, it's located just west of town. We arrive. Poplar trees line the drive with a reflecting pool to the left and the chateau right in front of us. Beautiful!

We walk in and inquire about a room. The caretaker of the estate whisks us up the huge leaning marble staircase. It's so crooked it's funny. The eccentric quirkiness fits our bill. We unpack our luggage, visit the outside gardens and walk around the property with the sun setting over the vineyards. We decide to stay for three nights. I ask and they respond. "Oui, oui." We're in!

We use St. Remy as a spoke on a wheel for day trips including Arles, Moulin de Daudet, Mouries, Eyguieres, Tarascon, Gordes, and Roussillon. We spend our first evening in St. Remy roaming through town. The town's design is quite unusual. It consists of three circles of buildings inside one another -- I can only assume for defensive purposes centuries ago. You're greeted with shops and restaurants on the outer circle, while residences are in the inner two circles. We feast on traditional French cuisine and relax with the local wine.

Morning is coming. The alarm goes off, it's about 4:30 in the morning. I told Kiki that I would be revisiting the grounds of the asylum, Sainte Paul De Mausole, where Van Gough's life tragically ended. The grounds of the asylum take you back in time to the 1880's with olive groves, fields of lavender and winding paths that Van Gogh, with his easel in tow, was able to capture the beauty all around him.

I quietly leave the Chateau Rousseau well before sunrise. I am determined to be at the asylum in plenty of time to set up my camera and record the sun rising over the mountain. Capturing the rays of the sunlight coming into the olive groves is my goal. I arrive ahead of time. I walk the grounds in the moonlight, quiet, contemplative. With empathy, standing here one can sense the turmoil in his life. He shot himself not far from this spot. Word was sent to his brother, Theo, who rushes from Arles and witnesses Vincent's last breath.

A little over a hundred years later and for a mere fifty-five million bucks, you can buy one of his paintings. Poor Vincent, never himself reaping the monetary rewards and dying a pauper while art dealers, museums and the like are laughing all the way to the bank. What would Vincent and Theo think? I think they would be really ticked off.

And so the story goes: after a tragic misunderstanding, Vincent, being financially supported by his brother for years, thinks he is being cut off monetarily due to Theo's growing family. Vincent, misunderstanding the meaning of a letter from Theo, goes out to the fields from where I stand and shoots himself in the head. Poor Van Gogh, nothing ever goes right. He lives a few days, mortally wounded.

Here comes the sun. A beautiful glow beams over the hill as I thought it would. As it rises, the light hits the olive groves with more brilliance than I had hoped. I got it!

Off to Arles we go. Arles is quite a large city with a Roman Coliseum. The day is cloud covered, not good for shooting photographs. We wind our way down some streets and Kiki is shopping away with a tablecloth in hand and some napkins. The fabrics are wonderful here. I, on the other hand, am on a mission. I go up the tower of the Coliseum to get photos of the town from above. Here I hope to find great vantage points of the rooftops, the streets, the river, the churches -- cloud covered and hazy -- not good. We then decide to hang out in a café and have a nice lunch while waiting in anticipation for the sky to open -- voilá, brilliant sunshine with puffy, cumulus clouds. I try in vain to engage the waiter to get the check -- to no avail. I try again. Sometimes they just don't get it. I try to embrace the beauty of taking one's time enjoying a meal and conversation, but at the moment I have a bigger fish to fry. I must capture this shot while I can. I get the waiter and off we go, back to the top of the coliseum. I show the lady my ticket from an hour ago and point to my camera. She lets me up for free and click, click and click. Mission accomplished.

Squirrels!! Kiki loves squirrels. Little brown ones with thin tails. I get some good photos of them too. We then realize that this is the first wildlife of any kind that we've seen on the trip. That's interesting. Back home, the animals are everywhere. There are three deer trails on the hill behind our house. We like to sit and barbeque and count the deer six, seven, eight and nine. I've even trapped groundhogs in my "Have a Heart" trap and subsequently moved them down to a state park so they don't eat my garden. I've also seen red fox cruising through the property. Flocks of wild turkeys visit while searching the ground for food and cleaning their wings with the dust from the dirt driveway. So with that said, where's all the wildlife in France? All I can assume is that they must have eaten them many years ago for survival during the wars. I wonder.

Lunch at the Van Gogh Café. This is a must for any painter visiting Arles. The restaurant has been painted in the same strange yellow that is in his paintings. It looks just like it did in the 1880's -- or at least how it looks in Vincent's paintings. The food was simple peasant food. It had some fancy stuff, but was set up to be authentic from Van Gogh's day. Yes, we hung out at a table sipping our cappuccino right under the wrought iron lamp just like in his paintings.

The following day, we made our way to Gordes and Roussillon up in the mountains north east of St. Remy. There we enjoyed great hiking and multiple vistas extending in all directions. Quaint and beautiful, our trip is beginning to wind down. Tomorrow we head back to Contignac, then to St Paul, the Niece airport and home. At this point, I've captured at least fourteen-hundred photographs. The times are changing, all digital. I'm early on the digital revolution. I'm up on the tech stuff. I've had my website since 1995. You snooze, you lose.

6 ITALY, THE RUN AROUND

First there was the exhibition in Laon, France, Paris, Provence and then Harry and his gallery. Now it's time for Italy with no agenda. This will be the first time in Italy for both of us. I think I've planned out an exciting agenda. Thankfully, my parents had been to Italy numerous times. Their information proved invaluable. We are, of course, winging it again. It has become the only way for us. The plane tickets are set and the car will be waiting for us in Rome, and that's it. It's like starting a new painting, a white canvas with nothing on it, all potential of what is to come. We are about to embark on a new trip with a blank canvas. Having no reservations allows you the freedom to change your direction at anytime.

Our agenda: grab the car after the flight into Rome, then head north into the hills of Tuscany, then the cities of Siena and Florence. We will then head up towards Venice, then back down to Cortona and into Umbria. The last leg of the trip will be Rome, and finally home.

We have become efficient travelers. We travel light with one regular bag between the two of us and our two carry-ons. That's it. Our flight is delayed and arrives late in Rome. We toss the luggage into the Fiat and take off towards Tuscany. We head north and stop in a little town to grab a bite to eat. I think we must have looked exhausted. It's the best pizza imaginable for tired eyes. We stay somewhere in town before heading to Montalcino. I must have been really tired, because I can't even remember the place we crashed.

After a good night's sleep, we arrived in Montalcino about ten in the morning. I spent quite a bit of time mulling over our travel books and checking things out on Google Earth. When I read about this town, it just struck a cord with me. We park the car and check it out. Wow, this little hilltop town is great. It kind of reminds me of Lambertville -- not in the architecture -- but rather that it is a small town with mom-and-pop shops. You can tell everyone knows everybody's name. This is my kind of town. I could live here, just like as in Lambertville. I feel very much at home.

I see a sign, Hotel dei Capitan. Let's check it out. Good location. We walk in and inquire "Camera?" -- the Italian word for a room with a view. The lady behind the desk scurries us up to room 301. Its view is fantastic. The room is not large, but tastefully decorated with a sunken bathroom and large French doors opening up to the east. We grab it. We then wander around town searching for the tourist office. When in Europe, look for the church steeple and nearby you will probably find the tourist office. Montalcino proved no different. With maps in hand, we are set to travel the surrounding towns of Pienza, Montepulciano, and San Quirico d'Orcia and wherever the wind takes us.

Let the exploration begin. We meander through the countryside with my camera shooting overtime. Before embarking on our trip, we thought it wise to watch the movie, "Under the

Tuscan Sun." Seeing the landscape in person is truly awe-inspiring. It's simply impossible for the big screen to do it justice.

I wake up in the morning around five a.m., my normal time. I brew some coffee. They have a small coffee maker in the bathroom. It's not cappuccino, but it will do and probably taste great. The sun is about to rise. I swing the French doors open looking to the east. The doors are from floor to ceiling and are about eight feet wide. They fold accordion style. The temperature outside is perfect, just a little cooler than the room. The queen bed is just across from the now huge opening to the vista. The sun is rising. The beauty before me, I can't even describe it. Grabbing my camera, I shoot. I shoot and I keep shooting. It's the most unbelievable sunrise that I've ever witnessed. I keep shooting, afraid to miss even a moment. It lasted a mere twenty minutes. I review the shots on the viewfinder to make sure I've got it -- relieved, I did. The coffee, it's almost room temperature now. I don't care, I drink it. It tastes great.

We move north to San Gimignano, the tower town. What a lovely town offering great architecture, restaurants, ceramic shops --

and gelato, oh, the gelato. On a hot day, gelato is fab. We then move on to Siena. The main Piazza del Campo, I'm convinced, is the best people watching spot on the planet. The Palio, it's a crazy horse race they set up in the plaza -- I haven't seen it -- heard about it -- and someday plan to be there for it.

Venice is a long ride. The superhighway is terrific; however, we opt for the mountain road. This windy pass to the west of the highway is a great drive. I now understand why the Italians think they are race car drivers. With a four-cylinder stick shift, the engine whining -- and remember, no breaks. You will notice the Italians don't break on curves.

We cross the bridge to the island of Venice at about eight p.m. We can't miss the big "**P**" for the parking garage on the building to the right. Venice is a pedestrian only city. We then park the car. We mull through our luggage and grab only what is needed for two days. We cross the street to catch the water taxi to our destination -- what a ride! We arrive at Saint Mark Square hungry. At this point, our blood sugar is surely low and we are famished. We grab the first café we run into. Frankly, we wouldn't have even cared if it was a McDonalds burger at this point. We just needed something. We are really getting spoiled. We have a great meal while hanging out at this quaint café just off Saint Mark Square.

We find a hotel along the way. It's nothing special. It's around midnight at this point, time to crash. The hotel was for only one night. They had nothing to offer for our second night. In the morning, I ask them for any other hotels they might suggest. They made a phone call. "One moment and we will move your luggage to the other hotel, if ok with you." As per their instructions, we head to the new hotel. I can't believe it. What a great find with huge windows opening up over a tributary to the main canal. I see a gondola winding a path in front of our window. It's a splurge -- oh, what the heck -- I'm not going to live forever.

We spend the entire day wandering around the maze of car-less streets. I shoot photo after photo. Everywhere you look, there's an image to paint: the architecture, the canals, the gondolas and the vistas across the sea to the other islands. The weather is spectacular. Once again, we are fortunate.

In the morning, I wake up at the usual five o'clock. I wander into the streets. It's so quiet, unusually quiet -- oh, that's right, no cars -- absolutely no cars, wow! I find a little shop just opening up. It caters to the local workers just arriving at the hotels. I get two cappuccinos to go. This is a complete cardinal sin here. However, they don't know the tradition of bringing the coffee to Kiki in bed. If they saw this, they would understand.

I arrive with the cappuccino. Kiki is smiling in bed, asking me about my wanderings around. I open the large windows to let the air in and enjoy the scene. I feel like a real Italian hanging out my window sipping my java and taking it all in.

I then see a man coming down the alleyway pushing a large cart. The cart is on two wheels. He balances it magnificently. Pushing it along, he drops it off at the dock below our window. He then turns around and walks from where he came and disappears. A few minutes go by -- yum, the cappuccino is excellent -- a boat rounds the corner and pulls into the dock down below my window.

Now I'm curious. There's a little crane on top of the barge -- how strange. I take another sip of java. I watch as the operator of the barge maneuvers the controls as he operates the little crane. The crane arm reaches to the left and above the cart and grabs hold of a hook on top of the container that's on the cart. The crane lifts it off the base up into the air and over the barge. Doors on the barge open up and the garbage drops in -- presto, garbage removal when you have canals instead of streets. This unique city, they've had to develop all kinds of ways to do everything. Surrounded by water, the canals are their streets. We came in on a waterbus. It all makes sense.

After Venice is complete, we trek down south to Cortona. We use the main highway this time. We are looking for speed and we get it. Christine falls asleep for most of the drive while I stay in the slow lane and go ninety miles per hour. If I weren't in the slow lane, I would get run over. If I drove any slower, I would be a danger on the road. Driving in France -- and so far in Italy -- you never see a policeman on the road. They definitely don't use tickets for revenue generation!

Arriving in Cortona in the mid afternoon, we enjoy a pleasant winding road to this hilltop town. One must park outside the town wall in a lot for tourists only. Parking in this town is restricted only to residents. Up we go, with just our carry-on bags. It's quite a steep grade climbing up to the square -- no gym needed here, walking these hills enables you to eat all the pasta you want.

The plaza is small but quaint with cafés, wine shops, restaurants and knick knack shops. We sit outside at a trattoria with cappuccino and a bite to eat. Trattorias are for grabbing a quick meal. I heard a joke once. What's the difference between a restaurant and a trattoria? Fifteen Euros.

On our walk up to the plaza, we passed a really posh hotel. We decided to check it out. It's a bit pricey. We request to see one of the rooms they have available. It's the biggest one I've ever seen in Europe -- or anywhere for that matter. It must be thirty by thirty-five feet. The king-sized bed looks like a postage stamp. Off to the left is a very large bathroom with a Jacuzzi. You then pass through a door onto a patio with a view looking west into the sunset. After taking the room, we sit out with our bottle of wine and some cheese that we picked up in the plaza. After an hour or so of watching the sun go down, while at the same time the lights of the town and valley start to twinkle like stars in the sky, we change our plans about going to Umbria. We will just have to save it for a trip unto itself. We decide to go back to Montalcino for a couple of days, then to an island on the coast and finishing up in Rome.

Across the valley we go. I commit a sin once again. I order due capuchini to go. I don't care. I know that we are supposed to take our time to sit down and relax in the square and chill -- but no, we want our mobile café. The poor person behind the counter can't seem to figure out what to do. They are not prepared for take out. They scramble and manage. We are off.

Kiki and I toss our bags into the Fiat and go. We meander down the hill looking for the house from "Under the Tuscan Sun" to no avail. Across the valley, we cruise the country roads through the gentle hills. I love driving through the countryside in the spring. Oh, the sweet smell of spring! We then come over a crest and -- bam! The poppy fields. Fields and fields of poppies. Everywhere you look, poppies all around -- poppies, poppies and more poppies.

We stop in the middle of the field and enjoy our portable cappuccino. What's better than this, sipping cappuccino in the middle of a poppy field? Now whose laughing at whom? If only the young lady at the café could see us now. We hang. We hang some more -- sweet! Off we go to Montalcino. We arrive back at Il Capitan and request room 301 and are informed, "Non. We have all filled tonight, tomorrow ok. Tonight have side room." We are pleasantly surprised to find out it's a separate apartment. We're good to go. We settle in, hit the pool and chill out. Eventually, we wander up to the café for a cappuccino. Staying in Montalcino for three days is very relaxing. I don't feel rushed. It's a good feeling.

We have plenty of time to experience the intimate details of life in Italy. We are now finding ourselves living more like the locals. We go to the market, hit the cheese shop and get in the groove with everyone else. I am able to get some serious photographing done. Each morning Christine and I take walks around town enjoying the slower pace of life. I can get used to this.

Christine and I then talk about the possibility of a painting trip in Montalcino in the future. My painting has been shifting from studio work to plein air. I used to work exclusively in the studio. I now work about sixty percent plein air.

I sit in our room at night and start planning. A plein air trip

-- I hadn't even conceived of such a thing before. The logistics would be difficult but not overwhelming. Wow, this could be very rewarding. A trip, go to one location and stay there with no running around, just hanging out and painting. What's the down side? What's the down side? Hmmm......

7 POSITANO

"The Pearl of the Amalfi Coast" is Positano. At my gallery in Lambertville, I spend quite a bit of time planning. I've done this before for Tuscany. However, from talking to folks and going on the web, I decide to take smaller panels and more of them. I believe the land and seascapes are suitable for this -- at least I hope so. It's all an educated guess.

We are now on plein air painting trip number two. The airline regulations have changed -- I need to adapt. What was once eighty pounds per bag is now fifty. This is a big adjustment. I switch to a thinner sixteenth-inch thick panel to conserve weight. I have one pair of shoes that are on my feet, three hiking pants that double as shorts, tee shirts, a few short sleeve shirts and one sweatshirt with a hood. And that's about it.

The packing, the flight -- and this time we have Chongo. We have his pet passport. His shots are up to date. Ten days before arriving in Italy, we visit the vet to get the appropriate paperwork completed. Chongo gets his examination to make sure he isn't frothing from the mouth. Alitalia is great with dogs. I was initially confused with their website, because it was the only airline that had no weight restrictions for dogs. When I first contacted customer service, the fellow was so nice. He replied to my query about weight restrictions in his heavy Italian accent, "What kinda doga do you hava?" I reply, "A Chihuahua." In his excitement he responds, "Oh, a little doga. Is no problema, no problema." We come to find out it's really true that, in Italy, dogs are family.

We leave for the airport crazy early. After we check the baggage, we relax at the airport and hang out at one of the restaurants. We like to make an event of it with plenty of time and no hurries with a glass of wine, and now we're ready for the flight.

We arrive in Rome. They are doing a lot of work at the

airport so the plane does not stop at the terminal. They bring a rolling staircase to the plane. We get off. I am very excited that we can now let poor Chongo out of his bag to do his thing. He's finally out. Round and round he goes, sniffing for the right spot like a little nut. I'm standing there and he won't take a whiz. I'm thinking to myself, "What, are you crazy? You're stuck in the plane all this time and you're going to be picky about your pee spot?"

We hop on the short flight to Naples, and before you know it we're there. The three of us work our way through customs and start heading out. Tired and anxious, our mission is now to spot our driver among the myriad of signs the drivers are holding, waiting in tow to connect with their rides. We finally spot "Gordon" -- so comforting.

We introduce ourselves to Claudio and off we go. From my google maps at home, I know the drive is about forty-five minutes. We drive south through Naples -- poor, poor Naples. I think to myself, this is kind of like Trenton, New Jersey. It's a city that comes close to making it, but never quite does. Our driver Claudio's English is quite good. I ask him various questions along our ride.

With Mount Vesuvius in the distance, we wind our way along the bay with various sites of curiosity. He then quips "Positano" -- "Excuse me, how did you say Positano?" Claudio answers, "Positano" pronouncing it with a long "O" like posing, posing for a picture. We are now twenty minutes from our destination, and now we know how to properly pronounce Positano -- with a long "O"!

The winding roads along the cliffs -- I don't normally get car sick -- maybe the combination of the flight, being tired and the winding road -- and I think Claudio is in a hurry for his next ride. I'm a bit woozy. We wind around a bend on the Amalfi drive and there it is, our first view of Positano. Nestled between the cliffs in its own little world sits this sweet little town. We can see everything along the coast towards Amalfi and up the mountains to the infamous "Walk of the Gods." Claudio takes a sharp right turn down a one-way street diving down switchbacks -- now I'm really feeling sick. Thank goodness I know we're almost there. Claudio hits the breaks just after a sharp curve and -- presto, there it is, Il Gabbiano, our home for the next six weeks.

We lug our stuff in. We arrive a little early for our check in time. They are a little flustered because they need more time to get our villa ready. "No problema," I tell Lucia. We hang out in the lobby with a bottle of chilled white wine relaxing at a table with this incredible view. With Chongo on my lap, Lucia's mother -- who is about seventy-five and absolutely no English -- brings Chongo a bowl of water. How sweet! "Grazie, grazie."

A short time passes and we take the elevator down to our villa. I notice the time is one p.m. I laugh, because we left our home in Lambertville at one p.m. yesterday -- twenty-four hours minus the six-hour time difference is eighteen hours door-to-door -- not bad! This includes getting to the airport ridiculously early, the flight, the transfer from Rome to Naples and the drive to Positano. The elevator drops us down into a cavernous hallway that opens up to the family gardens and our huge patio with the lemon trees. Bella!

We unpack, get settled in and venture out into our new surroundings. It's still fairly early and off we go through the wrought iron gate down the steps -- one-hundred twelve steps to be exact down to the road. If you ever visit Positano, be sure to bring good walking shoes -- and remember, lots of steps -- steps, steps and more steps. My walk down to the beach is the "shortcut" down the alleyway steps -- exactly five-hundred twelve to the beach. During the trip, I find myself doing this twice a day with my painting gear in tow, not to mention daily walking errands. In the Amalfi coast, you walk everywhere to do everything: groceries, post office, hardware store, etc.

We wind our way down the one-way road while passing shop after shop: ceramics, fish store, hotels, a café or two, jewelry and sandals. They are famous for making sandals here. We arrive at the church, Santa Maria Assunta. The whole town revolves around it, religiously, commercially, socially -- always an important part of Italian life. We make it to the final steps down through a narrow pathway under an archway and at the beach we arrive.

For the first time we get a good look at our surroundings and get our bearings. I had no idea the hills behind town were so immense. I knew there were hills back there, but I had no idea of how steep the grade was. The buildings really do climb up the hillside and are attached to the natural rock as part of the landscape. I guess that's part of what makes the Amalfi coast so beautiful.

We arrived on Saturday afternoon. After recovering from the flight on Sunday, we scope things out. First and foremost, where are the good painting spots? And, of course, where do I get a cappuccino in a fabulous café? Café Positano. The view from the tables right on the cliffs overlooking the town is spectacular.

Monday morning and the painting trip starts as in Montalcino. I'm standing in front of the Positano hardware store at nine o'clock in the morning. I walk in, and as per my friend in Montalcino, I ask "Trementina?" I know the containers are about quart size. "Due." She nods and that's it. I give her a few Euros and I'm off. That was much easier than in Montalcino. Maybe I'm getting the hang of this! By the time I walk back to our villa and get organized, its eleven o'clock. I'm off to start the first painting.

I head down to the beach, because it's obviously the focal point of town. I set up my easel, paints, brushes and so on. It reminds me of the vineyards of Tuscany -- not because of what I'm looking at -- but the process of creating the first painting on a trip. It's such a beginning, blank panels and all the potential. I look at them wondering what they will look like in a few weeks. Every day, one after another, I only have to think about painting. Nothing else. I wake up and only need to ask myself, where do I go painting? I grab a panel and off I go.

I'm on a mission. I have a goal of sixty paintings for the trip. A six-week trip allows five weeks' painting time. I lose two days becoming acclimated and getting turpentine. I also lose five days at the end of the trip. This allows the paintings to dry so I can pack them for the journey home. This means that I must complete two paintings a day, every day -- rain or shine. When we have an excursion to the Walk of the Gods or head to Capri or Amalfi, that eats into painting time. We use the last five days at the end to play tourist. I'm kind of burned out at this point, and we enjoy just relaxing.

I'm a week into my painting time. Fourteen paintings are done so far and I'm quite frustrated. It's not that I don't like what I've done, I do. However, it's been quite the struggle. I don't like to struggle with paintings because then the angst shows up in the finished painting. This was a problem I never anticipated. Painting last year in Tuscany was flawless, like painting in my backyard.

The light here in Positano is so different. Positano's light is completely harsh as a painter. As a tourist, its bright and strong. Standing out here with my easel it's very raw. That's the best word I've been able to come up with to describe it.

There's also something structural that was unanticipated painting here. Everything is in your face. Visually it all goes up at a forty-five degree angle. Bucks County landscapes go out away from you perceptively. Paris and Provence go out, Tuscany goes out. Positano, on the other hand, goes up like a wall in front of you.

It ends up taking me two weeks to get a complete grip on the scene. "Raw" is the word for the trip. Brutally raw color is what works on all the paintings. Sometimes I even skip my complimentary under painting. This will make it more brutal. And with the raw colors, it's a match. I begin to feel so much freer with the rest of the painting trip. Finally, I can relax.

We take our first day off from painting and we trek up to the "Walk of the Gods." I had previously gotten maps from the tourist office and studied them. I marked points of interest with my highlighter. We make sure to carry plenty of water and our hiking gear. We take Chongo out to do his duty, and then inside our flat for his afternoon nap. Christine and I head to the upper part of town where the tourists don't go. We grab some fruit at the veggie stand and up we go. We get to a very sharp curve in the road just before the huge sculpture of Saint Mary. We find an old sign leading the way to the "Walk of the Gods." Now we really start climbing up! The grade, at a number of points, gets ridiculous. The trail begins to get more wooded as we climb. There are some houses. Some are more like shanties with no electricity and no plumbing of any kind. These folks are really living off the grid. There's no taxman trekking up this mountain collecting anything. They have large gardens, chickens, peacocks -- lots of peacocks -- there must be some reason behind that. Water is not a problem. There are plenty of small creeks coming down the mountain. We weren't expecting to find this up here. We keep moving. The path kind of disappears and then we find it again. There looks like a clearing up above -- a house, it appears, as we get closer and the path leads right up to it. A dog starts barking madly. It's a big Rottweiler-type dog who's not happy right now. We turn around. Going back down the trail works great for us. No argument here.

Christine and I work our way down the path. Eventually, we leave the forest area into the upper part of town. One can tell that this is where the locals live. We stop at the only café, "Bar Internationale." We walk in and it feels like you're stepping into the 1880's. The locals are standing at the coffee bar gulping down their espresso. I try to get espresso once in a while but have never really acquired a taste for it. It tastes too much like sludge to me. Maybe some day I'll like it. Christine and I sit at a table that hasn't changed in ages. It's worn from the many decades of use with a patina to make the hosts of Antiques Roadshow jealous. After a long hike I get my usual, "What's the darkest beer you have?" The waitress names something. I reply "Si." Christine orders the house white. The drinks arrive. I can't see through the beer when held up to the light -- just what the doctor ordered! There's nothing like a dark beer after exerting one's self hour after hour. We get a small pastry to go with our drinks. We have some great conversation and pay the bill. By the time I get up, I'm stiff from sitting here after the long hike.

We then walk around and visit the little shops. The old men are hanging around chatting with each other as they do here. There's a wall by the bus stop which seems to be the congregation area. They hang out and catch up on today's news -- with a little politics thrown in -- and enjoy the evening with the sun setting over Capri. Not bad! We wander down into town and back to Il Gabbiano. Siesta time.

Where to go for dinner? We meander around and decide on a little restaurant up the road. We dine out with Chongo -- this is our routine. While dining, Chongo sits on my lap while I eat my meal. Chongo comes to all the restaurants with us in Italy. He comes into the grocery store, the shops -- anywhere we go, he goes. One time we arrived at a restaurant without him and the owner was quite upset with us. "Where's Chongo?" We explain, "He's tired from the day's adventures and is resting." The disappointment on his face says it all! Next time, we promise we'll bring the little guy.

This evening, the three of us arrive at one of our favorite restaurants on the Amalfi Coast, Bruno's. We both order the same meal, misto di mare -- or mixed seafood. The meal arrives -- fork in one hand and Chongo on my lap. Fantastico! We are hanging out at this place on the cliff with nothing but a little wrought iron railing between us and crashing down two-hundred feet to the beach. The view, as the sun drops down over the bay, is exquisite. We are talking about -- what, I don't know. Suddenly a voice chimes, "Hello. I don't mean to interrupt. I heard you talking -- what a cute doggie you have. My name is Francesco. My buddy's name is Ringo." His longhaired companion sits obediently at his side. I hadn't even noticed Ringo sitting at his owner's side. We strike up a conversation. We come to learn Francesco's an ex New Yorker -- it's a small world -- whose been living in Positano for about fifteen years. Francesco is a wealth of information about the area. I comment on how beautiful the islands are off in the horizon. He explains the history of how it was once owned by the Russian ballet dancer, Rudolf Nureyev. Nureyev's dream was to create a school for dancers. Unfortunately, he met his demise too soon to realize his dream. I then mention the interesting structures along the coast that look like mini forts -- and here comes the full-blown history. We come to learn that our new friend, Francesco, is a tour guide for the Amalfi coast.

Ravello comes up in conversation. Francesco offers us a tip to walk the main road, continue around the bend and through the tunnel to Atrani up to the plaza. Once arriving at the only café in town, walk through the archway in front of you into the caverns under the buildings. This is the path up the side of the ravine to Ravello. Here you will find one of the most spectacular hikes in all of the Amalfi Coast.

We start hiking up with our little dog in his messenger bag. Chongo was born with a deformed front left foot. Hence he needs to be carried on long hikes. Up we go through an area that is definitely less traveled. Here you will encounter simple houses clinging to the cliffs. I ask Kiki, "I wonder how they get their groceries home?" There's nothing but little paths. I suppose one could get a Vespa through with a basket on the back holding the groceries. We come across a small parking area. I can only assume they hoof it from there. Whoever lives here is in great shape.

We encounter a large abandoned building. It looks like an old school house -- probably years ago used for the local children in the hills. My, how times change. Now they probably catch a bus to Amalfi. We continue hiking up with lemon groves spanning both sides of the ravine. We come across a house being renovated --

bella! What a secluded spot they will enjoy with a view to die for. Their casa will be nestled between Amalfi and Ravello. Incredible.

My imagination gets the best of me. Could it be that an artist like Caravaggio is renovating this sweet find? Or is it perhaps an oasis for a novelist? Hmm. They are building terraced gardens for outdoor living with fresh vegetables at one's fingertips along with the aroma of fresh herbs waiting to be picked.

It then occurs to me that this is exactly what we've been doing at our house outside of Lambertville. I knew we were doing it, but it was more subconscious. Now it's out in the forefront. How can we further recreate our own little Italian-villa-lifestyle at home? I'll have to let this one gel in my brain and think about it.

Kiki and I continue up the last stretch to Ravello. It's been about a two-hour hike. We arrived at the main plaza and it's as picturesque as everyone touted. While wandering, a fellow is playing an instrument that I don't recognize. It's sounds like a cross between a harpsichord and a xylophone, with a little bit of a sitar mixed in. He's definitely playing ancient music that sounds very Mediterranean. I'm intrigued. I search for the sale of a CD -- none to be found. I'm disappointed. I make a point to purchase music on our trips. This will enable us to listen to the music we love from afar in our own backyard.

We find what looks like a quiet restaurant off the main plaza. We try to make it a point to get away from the tourist traps and savor the local Italian cuisine. You'll find that where the locals go, good food follows. I inquire about outside eating. He replies "Si" and gestures for us to follow him. Down the steps we go through a gorgeous dining hall with vaulted ceilings. We are then lead onto a back patio with an arbor filled with fragrant flowering vines of many varieties. The choice table offers a lovely breeze with flickering light bouncing off the leaves. He asks, "Ok?" I answer enthusiastically, "Si, si." The air feels refreshingly cool after the hike. Chongo sits on my lap. We order the local wine from Ravello and enjoy the process of going over the menu in anticipation of a well-deserved meal.

Francesco advised us to walk the grounds by the abbey offering spectacular views of the coastline. We are finding out quickly that advice from our new friend is right on the money. My camera is on overtime. Everywhere you look, your eyes are greeted with majestic vineyards, lemon groves, flowering gardens, vistas of the coastline and the crisp blue of the Mediterranean. We enjoy the rest of the day wandering through town. I venture into a gallery on the plaza. The quality of the artwork leaves something to be desired. This leads me to question the possibility of a gallery abroad brimming with artwork of the area: Ravello, Amalfi, Positano and Capri. The theme of lemon groves, vineyards and vistas of the coast would be a desired subject matter. I need to think about this. Looking around the plaza and being early in the season -- wow, look at all these tourists! With cash in hand, they want to take home a memory of their trip. It's all here, the pieces of the puzzle: my work, the association and the location. This applies for the whole of the Amalfi coast.

The last ferry back to Positano leaves at six p.m. -- I mean eighteen-hundred hours. Time will not allow us to hike back to Amalfi. Regretfully, we catch the bus. The bus stop is just a block or two from the plaza. We wait with the other tourists to get herded on for the ride down -- our only bus ride to date. Our choice of preference is walking and taking the ferries. It was pretty funny, though, as our bus rounded the final hairpin turn down to Amalfi all the while skirting traffic, cars, taxis, trucks and Vespas. Meanwhile, another bus is vying to squeeze past us -- all this on a road designed for horse and carriage! It took a few extra minutes with a couple of cars backing up and a car riding over the curb onto the sidewalk. They do have their own system -- and off we go.

The next morning, I wake up in our villa. It's time to make due cappuccini. It's in powder form from the local grocery store. Surprisingly, it's actually quite good. I prepare the java and when it's done I call out to Kiki, "Time to get up" -- it's actually a little bit of a joke between us. Back home, Kiki makes the breakfast and she calls to me, "Time to get up." I'm sitting waiting patiently at our table on the patio. In Positano one must have a patio. I sit under our lemon tree. With java in hand, all is good. Kiki then pops her head out the French door, "Is it cold out?" I answer, "Why don't you step out and see?" Kiki exclaims, "No, I'm not coming out. It's too cold!" Laughing, I respond, "For you or for me? It feels perfect. For you, get your sweater."

With breakfast in hand, our day begins waiting in earnest for the warmth of the sun to envelope our slice of paradise. While Kiki gets ready for the day I, on the other hand, check all my materials to make sure everything is in order: my supplies, paints, turpentine, palette, brushes, et cetera.

Now the big decision -- this is what I love about a painting trip. I only have two decisions to make every day. First, what size panel do I grab; second, where do we go for dinner -- that's it. There's nothing else to think about. There are no distractions, no mail to open, no lawn to cut, no gallery to run, nothing else. I don't mind those "distractions" at home -- they must be done -- without them, Positano could never happen. However, while on the trip, I have no concerns. I just grab a panel and off I go.

I'm off painting. With my Julian easel strapped to my back and my supplies in a bag over my shoulder, I head down the road from Il Gabbiano. The sun's strength is now a warm delight on my face. I discover a gem of a spot from which to paint. It's a postcard scene of Positano with a view overlooking the town, the coastline and the magnificent blue of the Mediteraneo.

My back now sighs as I unload the twenty pounds of

cumbersome supplies. I unfold my easel, lay out my supplies and here we are. With my blank panel in hand -- I so look forward to this part of the painting process. I have all this potential at my fingertips -- very exciting, indeed.

Looking over the scene, I realize that a fellow has parked himself just behind me over my right shoulder. His arms are crossed, watching silently. I ignore him. I start the painting by blocking in the shapes with my yellow ochre. He's still standing there. I begin the sky -- a brilliant warm blue. To do this, I create a warm orange -- the complimentary of the sky blue -- warm red, warm yellow mixed together equals warm orange. I lay down the underpainting. He's still standing there.

This isn't the first time that a local Italian has hung around for hours on end watching me paint -- I mean, the whole painting -- literally from setting up the equipment to its completion. They don't say a word. They're very respectful. I continue painting, layer upon layer. I can't help but wonder what he thinks as he sees the blue sky above him painted all orange. He doesn't leave. He just stands there not saying a word. I wonder what his mind is thinking. The painting is halfway done with all the complimentary colors finished. Next I start the sky with the "like" color. The blue sky now appears, then the green hill leading to the aqua Mediterranean -- ah, the light bulb moment -- my patient observer gets his reward. Now he understands.

We make the second decision of the day, where do we go for dinner? We decide on the Mediteraneo to fill our bellies. This will be our third experience with our new friends. Many of the restaurants are family run, Mediteraneo being no exception. The father, Enzo, is the owner. His two sons and daughter orchestrate the culinary pleasures. Kiki salivates in anticipation of the whole sea bass. I, on the other hand, order the tried and true misto di mare. Enjoying our meal, we witness the naiveté of an American couple ordering sea bass whilst not knowing the Italian dissection process that goes with it. Upon its arrival, the look on their faces is priceless. It's the whole fish, head, tail -- everything. The couple stares at each other with confusion. Their faces say it all. They whisper to each other, "What do I do with this?" She calls Arms over and jesters to have the fish filleted. You will find this is common practice that a waiter will bring a cutting board over and filet the fish in front of you. Arms, with no time to spare, quips, "I'm so sorry. When in Rome, do as the Romans." He swiftly walks away. I'm somewhat stumped. I've never seen this request refused before. The American couple stares at each other. She is quite disturbed with her lips pursed. He shrugs his shoulders, grabs his fork and knife and starts digging in -- what a trooper. She, on the other hand, looks at her plate in disgust and spends the evening picking at it. She doesn't debone it in anyway. She just stabs it with her fork periodically. Quietly, we chuckle to ourselves.

Christine, to the contrary, has become an expert at filleting fish. I showed her twice and that was all she needed. When presented with a whole fish, Kiki chops the head off, then the tail and with one slice, from head to toe, fillets it. She pulls out the spine and it's done in twenty seconds, with not a single bone left behind! She's truly a waiter's dream.

In the evenings, we do the Italian thing and walk around town enjoying the evening. A week or so later we spot "Arms" with both arms up in the air looking rather odd. Upon closer inspection, we witness his failed attempt to make a call on his cell with his fingers wiggling madly in the air. We walk up and -- "Wholly cow, what happened?" With both his arms pointed up in the air wrapped in casts, he answers, "I had Vespa accident. I was going around curve and another Vespa going too, too fast and we -- boom handlebars and off I go into air." I tell him, "You're so lucky you didn't hit your head. It could have been so much worse." He explains to us there are seven pins in his left arm. It's a very serious break. I think to myself that could have been his head. He's a very lucky fellow indeed. "Arms" explains that he has to keep his arms elevated for six weeks so they can heal properly. He doesn't know how he will sleep at night and I have to admit that Kiki and I can't remember his real name. However, when we refer to "Arms" we know exactly whom we are talking about.

Our trip is winding down. We meet with Francesco at one of the cafés. The night ends with us discussing the possibility of future exhibitions at different hotels, alternative spaces or maybe even a gallery in Positano! Francesco is as excited about the possibilities as we are. I love this kind of brainstorming. People with ideas can move mountains. I have a lot of thinking to do -- a whole lot of thinking.

It's our last day in Positano for painting. We will still be here for about five days while waiting for the paintings to dry. I'm almost at my goal, fifty-six paintings so far with four to go. I'm determined to reach sixty paintings. I must do four today. After breakfast I head down the five-hundred and twelve steps to the beach. I do a painting of the bay with the fishing boats. I then hike up to our villa and realize that I need three more paintings to reach my goal. How to do this? I get to our villa and ponder -- of course, it's right in front of me -- the lemon trees. I've painted them before a couple of times on this trip and they're a joy to paint. This is my solution. With ease I playfully create three paintings of lemon trees under the Mediterranean sun. I've got my Italian tunes on the headphones and just go at it. You can't think. It just has to be instinct. Paint, paint, paint. The only thing that slows me down is mixing the paints.

Six weeks -- that means five weeks' painting time. My goal each day is simply exploring and capturing in oils the beauty before my eyes. What a beautiful thing. We're so fortunate that this is something we've been able to make a part of our lives. The majority of people who travel this length of time are retired. We have found a way to do it while we're still young and vibrant. Economically, we would be foolish not to do it. How fortunate we are, indeed.

8 THE BEGINNING

I think I was in the sixth grade. I was over at John Christaldi's house, and it was raining out. What are we going to do? We played some board games but soon got tired of them. John suggested that we draw. I had kind of gotten into drawing and had a lot of fun doing it. John got some paper and pencils. We just started drawing. I drew my sailing and pirate ships, the perfect subject for an eleven-year-old boy. We finished. We both held up our drawings to show each other. I didn't know it then but it was a "light bulb" moment for me. My drawing wasn't just a little better than John's, it was a lot better. Even he was surprised. "You've gotten good," he said. I replied, "I don't know. I've just been drawing a lot." I had surprised even myself.

You see, John was the artist, not me. How could my drawing be better than his? John then said, "Lets draw comics." He had these funny caricatures that he drew in the past. I had followed suit and kind of made up my own little comic strip. John and I drew for quite some time. I could tell he was working hard to redeem himself. "Ok, finished?" We then exchanged papers to get a closer look at what the other had done. It happened again. "Wow" I thought to myself, "I really can draw better than John, the artist." From that day on, I thought of myself differently.

My parents were extremely instrumental in encouraging me with my art interests. As a matter of fact, they were fabulous with all four of us kids -- from sports, music lessons, art lessons -- any interest any one of us had, we got lessons. I don't know how my mom survived driving us everywhere, day after day, year after year -- times four -- or how my dad managed to pay all those bills. For example, I can remember Nancy playing piano, all the while Mark with drums and clarinet; Lynn, piano and violin; and me with stand up bass. Mind you, this doesn't include that we all had tennis lessons. And also don't forget there was soccer, basketball, field hockey and much more. I would also have my oil painting and watercolor lessons.

I found I was influenced most by the watercolor lessons. My parents knew of a lady through the church who taught adult watercolor classes in the basement of the local art supply store. Her name was Nat Lewis. My mom called Nat and she made an exception for me since I was only thirteen. We had gotten a list of art supplies to get: Windsor Newton watercolors, the Pike palette, arches hot press watercolor paper, and specific brushes. I was so excited. Once a week for ten weeks was the standard session.

I arrived the first day. Nat introduced me to everyone. It seemed that most had already taken lessons from Nat before. To my surprise, Mrs. Newsome, the mother of a good friend in school, was also one of the students. The class was a simple format. Nat would demonstrate a painting scene and we would follow along step-by-step along with her instructions -- and, shall I say, the tricks of the trade in trying to control this wild medium. I had a blast and I think the adults -- mostly ladies -- got a kick out of this little kid who loves to paint. It doesn't take me long to realize that I have more in common with these adults than my friends at school. The ten weeks go by in a flash. Eventually I do another ten weeks with Nat, which leads to ten weeks with Ed Havas, then another ten with Ed -- the list goes on -- I'm hooked.

I, along with my siblings, are heavily involved with playing tournament tennis all over the place. My poor mom running around like crazy. This is something one doesn't appreciate until later in life -- all the sacrifices. My brother, Mark, and I had been going to a three-week overnight tennis camp for a couple of years now. My older sister, Nancy, even became ranked in the E.L.T.A. (Eastern Lawn Tennis Association) and taught tennis at a racquet club. Mark and I both ended up with knee problems. Off to the doctors I go, and basically I'm sidelined for now.

Mom and Dad, on the other hand, were planning a vacation in Maine for two weeks in the summer all by themselves. Nancy was teaching tennis, us boys were at tennis camp and Lynn visiting a childhood friend for two weeks. They were probably shocked that with four children they were going to have two whole weeks by themselves -- well, the best laid plans! Little me, the youngest, got sidelined from the knee problems with no tennis camp -- what to do? Well, they couldn't leave me home alone. I was too young. With no alternatives, they asked me if I wanted to join them in Maine and bring my watercolors. I was thrilled. Off we went. I brought my art supplies and the camera I got for Christmas.

I had never been on a trip like this before. It was all so new. We stayed in a cabin in Port Clyde, Maine for about a week, then Bar Harbor for the other week. Of course, we did day trips all over the place with my camera and watercolors in tow: Mohegan Island, Kennebunkport, Acadia National Park. It was fantastic. It was so different from home.

Best of all, as I look back, it was a time when I actually got to know my parents -- I mean, really got to know my parents -- with a chance to hang out and talk about all kinds of things without the hustle and bustle of school, homework, sports, three other siblings and all the distractions of everyday life. I was about fourteen on vacation with just me, mom and dad. It was one of the best vacations of my life.

After the trip, my mom began to have difficulties with her eyes. I didn't understand at the time what the problems were -- I was just a kid -- and in those days we were kept in the dark about such matters. What I do know is that I would get taken out of school to escort my mom to the eye doctors in New York City. I would wait for hours in the doctor's office. When she came out, her eyes would be dilated and teary. It would be a couple of hours before she could drive home. As a result, we would hit the museums.

We would walk out of the doctor's office and go to the Met, the Whitney or the Guggenheim. Depending on what exhibits were going on, we might even hit a couple of them. Many of the exhibits left a lasting impression on me. The Alexander Calder exhibit at the Whitney -- I thought what fun things -- these mobiles are so playful. They must be so fun to build. Then as we were leaving the museum, a worker was up on a large stepladder changing the sign. He was adding Calder's death date of 1976. I didn't know he had just died. I realized then for the first time you don't have to be dead to have your art in a museum. I had always thought of museums as a resting place for dead artists' work. It was a good day. I had learned many things.

I also remember an exhibit by Duane Hanson. I had no idea about his art. Mom and I went up to the third floor of the Whitney to meander around. The elevator door opened up, we walked in and there's nothing on the walls. We ventured into one of the large exhibition spaces. There were lots of people roaming around looking at nothing. What are they doing? There's nothing here, nothing on the walls, no sculpture -- nothing. I thought to myself, "These people are kooky. How did that homeless lady get into the museum?" There was a fat lady in a bathing suit lounging on a beach chair as if she's at the beach -- oh my! Then I realized that these people were sculptures. I had never seen anything like it. People were positioned in everyday life situations -- trompe l'oeil, fooling the eye. The one I liked best was the museum guard. I thought that was perfect. We had gotten off the elevator and there he was standing, not moving, with his head down sleeping. My eye fooled. Only upon leaving did I realize that the guard wasn't a guard but, rather, a sculpture!

It was about this time that my uncle Hamilton died. Everybody in the family called him "Ham." Ham will never know what a big impact he had on my life. When Ham was ill with cancer, we would visit him. I would bring my drawings, cartoons and watercolors. Ham was an artist. He was what you might call a weekend painter. He worked in his family's marble polishing company, but he was a gifted artist. Figure drawing and watercolor were his favorite medium. Ham passed away and then suddenly boxes and boxes of his art supplies arrived at our house. I think there must have been twenty-five boxes.

I had set up a little studio space in the playroom next to the piano. With my own money from cutting neighbors' lawns, I bought a drafting table to work on. There was a set of shelves to my left for my art supplies. It wasn't just art supplies that arrived in those magical boxes, but books, at least fifty books on art. These books were my guide on how to draw hands, feet, heads and figures. They also included information on perspective, watercolor and oils. There were even art history books. I had a whole library at my fingertips.

I would spend thousands of hours copying pictures from the books: a Wyeth watercolor, Venus on the half shell, a painting by Vermeer, figure drawings and the like. These resources, at my fingertips every day, were the best thing that could have happened to me. Art became my life. This is when I knew that someday, somehow, I would become an artist.

Creativity was encouraged in our house. Dad was an architect. Mark, my brother, knew when he was five that he would also be an architect. He now has his own successful architecture firm. I have early memories of my dad teaching me one, two and three point perspective at the kitchen table, all the while giving me assignments on using them. Dad always did work for his architecture firm in the evening while the Carol Burnett show was on. Rolls of yellow trace paper were used to scribble changes in his designs -- layer upon layer -- scribble, scribble -- scratch, scratch.

My brother Mark and I would constantly sneak into his desk and grab some markers and paper. Mom always thought we would work for Hasbro or another game company. We were always building our own games from scratch: the boards, the game pieces, the rules -- everything, top to bottom.

Forts were the mainstay of activity in the woods around our house. At one point, I counted eight. The largest tree house was three stories tall. Mark designed and supervised the building. He actually built most of it. My mother was concerned with how big it was getting and wanted dad to check it out structurally. Dad, with his architecture and engineering degree, gave it a big thumbs up. It had electricity, a shingled roof, deck, tables, chairs and game room and, yes, Mark did become an architect.

It didn't stop with forts. Across the street there was a stream that we constantly dammed up so we could sail our handmade toy boats. They sailed, caught fire and sank in battle. Yes, we were very realistic. Don't even begin to ask me about the tank battles or the blackened soot stain on the garage ceiling -- I have no idea how it got there -- that's my story and I'm sticking to it. And, no, my parents had no idea.

9 THEY ALL SAID

"You want to become an artist, that's nice. What do you plan to do to make a living?" I must have heard this a thousand times when I was a kid -- so negative. In reflection, I wonder how many of those people ever took a chance in life with the risk of failure. They played it safe. They got their secure paycheck. And when they become old in a nursing home I wonder if they'll ask themselves, "Why didn't I follow my dreams? Why didn't I take a chance?" Without taking a chance, dreams cannot be realized.

The other comment I loved was, "That will make a nice hobby. How are you going to make a living?" Even when I was at

RISD, the number one art school in the country, I heard it over and over. "Oh. So what are you going to do after school, illustrate? What are you going to do to make a living -- you know, eat?"

All people think about is Van Gogh. He was a pauper who cut off his ear. He was poor, miserable and nuts. Are there some artists like this? Of course. I also know of some lawyers who hate the work they do, wish they could get out of it but have huge student loans they have been paying off for years -- poor and miserable.

There are also plenty of wealthy artists. Let's take John Singer Sargent as an example. In 1908, he was making one-hundred thousand dollars per portrait. In today's dollars that's equal to about two-million, three-hundred thousand. Have you ever been to Monet's studio in Giverny? How about Remington, Dali or Andy Warhol? There are also countless artists who have made an excellent living whom you've never heard of. For example, you haven't heard of little old me. I've had my own gallery exclusively showing my work for nineteen years now. My wife, Christine, and sister-in-law, Donna, work for me. Donna is especially invaluable. Along with manning and selling at the gallery during the week, she handles the prints, framing, computer work, web site, emails, phone calls and lots of other day-to-day business and, of course, the gessoing. She likes to say that it all starts with her, and it's completely true. This frees me up for doing what I do best, which is to paint.

Christine is the frame carver. We make hand-carved frames for the oil paintings. I build the structure. Christine is the only one with the patience to do the carving, and then Donna or I do the gold leafing and finish work. However, now that we've done renovations at our house, Christine will have improved studio space to do the leafing and finish work. It's a family affair.

10 THE POOR STARVING ARTISTS' SYNDROME

I am by far not the only one who does well. A fellow who owns a gallery next door to me with his work exclusively sold an incredible five-hundred fifty paintings last year -- you don't know his name either. Another artist opened her gallery in Lambertville and in the first year had a nice six-figure income. Again, you don't know her name. Another friend of mine opened a gallery with his fine art photography. After a few years, he bought the building out of the photography sales and is there only on weekends.

On the flip side, I know artists who love to be poor -- that may sound funny, but it's true. If you sell, you're selling out. If you don't sell your artwork, you're true to your work and pure. I call it, "The Poor Starving Artists' Syndrome." They perpetually shoot themselves in the foot over and over again. And then they complain they have no money, their work is misunderstood, or that the public isn't ready for their kind of work -- excuses, excuses, excuses. If Christo can wrap an island or building with plastic and make a fortune, you can do any kind of work and make a living at it if you want to -- that's the key, you have to want to.

What does that mean, "You have to want to"? If you want to be a poor starving artist, I have the perfect solution. First, don't let anyone but a few friends see your work. To let potential customers see it would be selling out. Next, make sure that you keep your work in the studio hidden and not in galleries. Why not only do a handful of pieces each year with the price so high no one will buy them? Then do work that has no emotional connection or relevance to anyone's life. If you have to explain your art, it has failed to its core. It would be like a comedian explaining a joke. If you have to explain it, it simply doesn't work.

I had an artist in my gallery at one point, and a potential

customer walked in and was inquiring about a few paintings. She

had swatches with the colors of her couch, wallpaper, window

treatment, etc. After she left the artist said to me, " Doesn't that just

drive you crazy? I wouldn't be able to stand it with her stupid

swatches matching colors. She doesn't care about the paintings one

bit." I then asked this artist what her favorite piece of art in all of

history is. She gave me the name of some obscure painting that I

barely remembered from my art history courses. I then replied, "Oh,

you mean that commission for the lady with the swatch?" She

looked at me with a puzzled look on her face. "What do you mean?"

I answered, "That piece of artwork that's your favorite in all of

history, didn't you know that it was a commission for a lady with

swatches of her couch color?" She was puzzled for a moment. She

then asked me if I taught.

I explained further to her, "Look, that lady is dead." She

looks at me puzzled again. "What do you mean?" I exclaim, "Dead,

dead, dead! That painting will outlive her. She's about sixty, and in

about twenty-five years she's room temperature. Her kids will fight

over the inheritance. One of them gets the painting. He then sells it

to a dealer for far too little, just because he wants the cash. The dealer puts it in an auction house and sells it for fair market value to someone who just loves it for all the right reasons. They die. With no kids, the estate gets auctioned off and another dealer, for his personal collection, buys it. He's buying it only as an investment. He dies. So on and so on." In other words, each painting will carry with it a life of its own.

What I want is their money. This way I can keep painting full time, all the time. I can live in a nice house. I can hire people to work with me. I can travel and go exploring and capture paintings from all over the world. Sure, I enjoy my customers at the gallery. Many of them have also become good friends over the years. We all have our agendas. For some, it might be the swatch and matching the couch. Or maybe the painting of the river reminds them of fishing with dad who is long gone. Or the forest's leaves takes them back to walking through the woods as a young child. Maybe the winter scene reminds them of growing up in Vermont with the smell of the cozy wood burning stove.

If I don't sell my paintings, I can't hire anyone -- less painting. If I don't sell my paintings, I have to get a "regular" job to pay the bills -- less painting. If I don't sell my paintings, I won't be a full-time artist -- less painting.

If I paint more, my work will improve year after year. When someone brings in their swatch, most of the time they're a little embarrassed, while adding, "I know I shouldn't be matching the couch, but I can't help it." I put them at ease with a reassuring, "No problem. I do the same thing at my house. Let me see your colors." I will then go around my gallery holding up the swatch to various paintings while asking about her wall colors, the furniture and style of the house.

If I can't find something in the gallery that works, I'll chat with them about commissions. I explain, "I'll take your swatches, tack them to the wall next to my easel and work the colors in. It doesn't matter to me, I use color theories. You just have to worry about the image you like." I will then take her over to the hundreds of prints available in my gallery while explaining, "Just pick out the images you like and we can go from there. I can make it in any size you want. I know how difficult it is to find the right image with the perfect colors and the right size to boot." She nods her head up and down. "I've been looking for almost a year!"

I've just solved this woman's problems. I let her know that the usual time commissions are finished is six to eight weeks -- but that's not guaranteed. It will be done when it's done and when I'm satisfied. I may even be halfway finished, and if I don't like the way it's progressing, I'll scrap it and start all over. Perfection takes time. They're so happy with this. She knows her size, pulls out her checkbook and writes the check for half. For commissions I do half up front, and half when they pick up the finished piece.

Commissions -- I love commissions -- guaranteed money. What comes with commissions is often even better than the money. You are often forced to do things that you would never do on your own. We're all creatures of habit. It's so easy churning out the same kind of thing over and over again. Commissions, on the other hand, open up new ideas and new directions for your work. For example, I did a commission for a couple who live on a lake. They walk the trail around the lake every morning after coffee and before going to work. They wanted two paintings, each from opposite ends of the lake for above their couch. Fine. We discussed approximate sizes. I then drove to the lake to take photographs. I normally work plein air, but have found for commissions it usually works better for me to work from photos. From one end of the lake, the trail is on top of an earthen dam. Excellent. The lake is beautiful. I arrive at seven a.m., the same time frame they walk. I then go to the other side of the lake. It's wooded with lots of scrub brush and vines. A great trail to walk but nothing to paint. I keep searching for something of interest to paint. Nothing.

We have a meeting at the gallery to go over my photographs to make final decisions on the paintings. After showing them the photos, they nod in agreement about the one side of the lake with nothing to paint. I then pitch to them the only thing I could think of. I offer a single long panoramic. The photos from on top of the dam were conducive to a long horizontal. We agreed that the final dimensions for the painting should be 12 x 56 -- framed 18 x 62. I would have never thought to do this proportion on my own. Another example of stretching one's self through a commission. It covered the same space on their wall above the couch just as the two paintings would have together. As a result, I have two very happy customers. They write the check.

On the other hand, some artists feel that doing commissions lessens their credibility. Hence, they lose the opportunity to think outside the box while at the same time enhancing the "Poor Starving Artists' Syndrome." When I first opened my gallery, I would do a commission of anything. Let my dream of painting full time and having a gallery of my own paintings go down the drain because I don't feel like painting something? How shortsighted would that have been?

Early on, a couple from Princeton had a tiny photo of an abstract painting. They loved the colors and shapes and they were seeking an artist to reproduce it in oil. It was obvious that they had been turned down many times. I could just hear the artists responding, "I don't copy other artists' work," or "That's not my style of artwork that I do," or "These rich people from Princeton think they can force me to paint anything." They described their space that the painting was to go in. It was a large wall, twelve feet high on one side and about twenty feet high on the other with skylights throughout. I asked them if I could come over to measure the space and get a feel for their environment. They were so excited. This is so simple. It's called "customer service."

Arriving at their home, I delight at the prospect of being in the company of their eclectic art collection consisting of five feet tall Ming Dynasty vases, to a traditional seventeenth century European still life and ending with some Pop art. While talking about the project, I come to find out that every six months or so she rearranges the whole art collection. This way the art never gets stale and she can enjoy every piece in a new light. I think to myself, "How is that for enjoying one's art collection!"

I let them know I will work up a sketch so they can see what they'll get before I go ahead and start the paintings. A few weeks later we meet and I make the proposal of not one painting but three for that huge wall -- not three square or rectangular paintings, but rather three pieces that fit together like a puzzle and not one right angle in any of them.

At her whim, the paintings can be put together in different arrangements. They can be hung separate, together -- any arrangement you want. It's designed to change over time. The scope of the project tripled, as did the price tag. It didn't matter to them. They were thrilled. When completed, I brought the paintings over and hung them. Happy customers, just the way I like them. This one project paid for our entire trip to Provence. I probably did about two-hundred paintings of southern France and sold every one of them. You do the math.

One rather comical thing that happens frequently at the gallery is the throng of artists who come in and tell me how to paint and run my gallery. Inevitably, I find out they don't paint full time, they're a bartender so they can pay the bills or paint mostly for themselves. They also tell me, "People wouldn't understand my work." They don't have time to be bothered dealing with galleries. Another excuse I hear is, to sell they would have to change their work -- you know, the old "painting barns" thing.

If I have customers in the gallery, I won't even deal with these "artists." If there are no customers in the gallery, I'll explain to them that they have it all backwards. I love the look on their faces.

"What do you mean 'backwards'?" I'll counter, "Think about it. You come into my gallery and start criticizing my work like you know what you're doing." They counter, "I'm entitled to my opinion." Again I add, "Yes, you're entitled to your stupid opinion. What you're saying is that I should take your advice, and what? I should become a part-time painter like you, so I can work a regular job to pay the bills while taking away from my painting time? So what you're saying is that I should be a poor starving artist just like you? Maybe I should close my gallery because you think it's commercial dealing with the public, or below me to be selling my own work? Maybe I should be poor like you so I can cancel my painting trips to Europe. What in your mind makes you think that I would be interested in your opinion, let alone take your advice?"

If they were smart and used the other side of their brain, they would be coming into my gallery picking my brains about how I do it. They usually leave dumbfounded, because they can't think outside of their little box -- the box they were taught in art school. They'll keep doing things the same way they've been doing for years, expecting the results to change. It won't. "The definition of insanity is to keep doing the same thing over and over again and expecting a different result." That quote came from Albert Einstein.

11 RISD

The mail came, a letter from the Rhode Island School of Design, RISD (pronounced "RIZ-dee") I was seventeen, and it was a thick letter. I knew I was in. It only takes one piece of paper to say, "No, thank you." RISD was my first choice of colleges. I had gotten into all five colleges I applied to: Parsons, School of Visual Arts, Philadelphia College of Art, some school in Massachusetts I don't even remember and RISD. My mother and I visited each college personally to see firsthand if it would be a good fit. She did this for all four of us kids -- I know God will bless her. The fact that I got accepted into all five of my choices still amazes me even to this day.

My parents never quite came out and said it, but it was understood that the world was at our fingertips. Any school we could get into, they would find a way. I was the last of four kids in college and the most expensive. My dad's architecture firm had taken off a number of years earlier making this possible. The poor man had kids in college from 1973 through 1984 -- eleven years. At its peak, my dad had three of us in at the same time. Dad worked incredibly hard for so many years. My parents made a great team. They provided to the fullest each child's dream, made possible by the fruits of their hard labor.

My dad was a fighter pilot in WWII. He never talked about his service, like so many from this time. I remember helping my dad clean up his den when I was about ten. In the bottom drawer, there were a bunch of old family photos. I was perusing through them and came across one that peaked my curiosity. The photo was of seven men wearing leather jackets standing in front of a plane. I asked him, "What's this?" Dad points to one of the men and adds, "That's me in Texas in front of our training plane." I'm puzzled. "But Dad, that's a biplane. It's not from WWII." He laughs and explains, "The good planes were all out in the field. As soon as they were manufactured, they were shipped to Europe or the Pacific. There were no spares for training, so we used what we could get our hands on. Besides, most of our training was done in books." I question, "What do you mean, 'books'?" Dad then scrounges around the shelves behind his desk and pulls out little books. He opens them up and shows me the flight patterns with all sorts of diagrams for this purpose and that. They were filled with written notes all looking very Greek to me. He explains that they didn't have much gasoline and that what they had went out to the soldiers overseas. Dad only had six hours of solo flying time before he was shipped out on the aircraft carrier. I was completely amazed. Just six hours and off you go.

Dad was a risk taker -- a calculated risk taker. He planned and figured everything out to the last detail. After the war, dad was on the GI bill. He graduated from the University of Michigan with a degree in architecture. He was rewarded with a job at a large architecture firm in Newark, New Jersey. He worked himself up to project manager with numerous architects under him. After he had been with the firm for ten years he, along with another architect in the firm, decided to break out on their own. My mother gave him her unconditional support. I don't think too many wives in 1961 would have given such support especially with three young children and me in the oven.

One of the reasons I think Dad was willing to give up the security of a "regular" job was that his father was just the opposite. Grandfather worked for the State of New Jersey in a comfortable job. While in the Great Depression, he still received eighty percent of his salary. They were doing very well. An opportunity then arose in which he could have been one of the four founders of an insurance company. He turned it down -- a missed opportunity. It later went on to become Prudential Insurance Company.

Dad gave great advice when I was a teenager. The first was about what to do when I grow up. He said, "Do what you love to do. If you do what you love, you will work hard at it. If you work hard at it, you'll improve and the money will follow. And always remember, it's the process that matters. The journey is where you must find the joy!"

The other piece of advice that sticks out is, "Money isn't everything. Without your health, you have nothing. Yes, money isn't everything, but it sure is nice not to have to worry about it."

My Mother was enrolled at the New Jersey College for Women. She paid her own way by working summers as a waitress at the Jersey Shore. Just before the war broke out, she was involved with a cultural exchange seminar to improve relations between the U.S. and Japan. Just days before the seminar, Pearl Harbor was attacked. Growing up during the depression and WWII, in various ways, defined both my parents.

I took my S.A.T. tests, got the results, and was crushed. "I can't be that stupid," I thought to myself. How can this be? I'm a good student. True, I'm not the best test taker, but I think I have a decent brain in my head. With these scores, I'm going nowhere. Thank God I wanted to go to an art school. They all require "special admissions." That means a portfolio of twelve pieces, plus three drawings to their specifications. I had to knock their socks off. The portfolio I had been working on for some time was all set. I hired my cousin, a professional photographer, to shoot my work and paid him quite well. The slides came back and they were terrible. I couldn't believe it. I then decided the only way to do this right was to do it myself. Dad and I went to 47th Street Photo in New York City to buy a camera. My first camera was a Pentax K1000. What a workhorse. I used this camera until the digital revolution some twenty-five years later.

I shot everything over again. The exposure wasn't quite right. I shot it again. The colors were off. I had to make a filter adjustment, then a film tweaking which led to a light bulb wattage change. With a little trial and error, I got it. Perfect. Now I can shoot my work forever. I laid everything out for the twelve pieces of work and shot them. The film came back and it was perfect.

Next came the drawings. Each school I was interested in required three drawings. For RISD a drawing of shoes, a bicycle and an optional drawing. Knowing my S.A.T. scores were lacking, I knew I had to excel above all the others. For the drawing of the shoes, I decided, I must do something unusual. I did the drawing as if you were inside the shoe looking out like it's a cave. The second one was a close up of the gears on my ten-speed bicycle. My optional drawing was a two-dollar bill appearing to come out of a blank piece of paper into three dimensions with every detail -- all the while fooling the eye. In the end, I was accepted into the five colleges I applied to. I'm sure that when the admissions staff saw my S.A.T. scores, they must have gotten a good laugh.

12 RISD, THE EXPERIENCE

My brother, Mark, drove me to RISD in my parents' Chevy Chevette. It was packed to the gills. Here I am, an eighteen-year-old freshman, at what's heralded as the finest art school in the country. I'm determined to work 24/7 for the first month or so. I figured that if I gave it at least one-hundred ten percent and didn't make it, at least I couldn't blame myself for not having given it my all.

About three weeks into my RISD experience, I knew almost no one. I had been a hermit. I went to class, ate in the dining hall, then back to my dorm room where my drafting table was set up for all the projects. I didn't sleep much the first three weeks. I managed to catch catnaps here and there. One-hundred ten percent right from the start. Three weeks passed. I survived. Frankly, I was a little surprised at first.

Freshman year consisted of drawing, two-dimensional design, three-dimensional design, English and art history. Everyone gets lumped together: painters, sculptors, architects, graphic designers, glass blowers, light metals, etc. This schedule was typical of most art schools.

The drawing and dimensional classes were a ton of work, but not a problem for me. I aced all three of them both semesters freshman year. I found myself having problems with the liberal-arts-end-of-things. The English, I barely remember. I just squeaked through it and that was it. The art history, on the other hand, was just the opposite. I found it invigorating. I was blessed to have had Dr. Kirshenbaum as my professor. His lectures were riveting, from art's inception featuring Venus of Willendorf circa 23,000 BCE through modern art. I had him in the main lecture hall with everyone else and in the classroom as my individual professor. I knew it was going to be tough -- really tough. As a result, I joined three study groups to repeatedly go over the volumes of material. I studied like I've never studied before or since.

I took the midterm and it went well. I was relieved. I figured I got a solid B -- I'd even be happy with a B-. All is good. The following week the test was handed back with the results. This must be a mistake. I rechecked the name on the top. This has to be someone else's test -- no, that's my name. My mouth is open in disbelief. I received an "F" with a score of thirty-seven. How could I get a thirty-seven when I studied harder than any time in my life? If I had just partied and skipped classes, sure, a thirty-seven would make sense. This does not make sense.

Well, as it turned out, half the class failed the test. There was one "A" from a third-year transfer student from Yale who was an art history major -- which meant no curve. We spent the class going over the test and I found my error. I was regurgitating the material verbatim. He wanted thinking responses. He was looking for your thoughts on the material in connection to the world around us.

There was just the final and class participation to make up for the thirty-seven. I ended up with a "D." I never thought I'd be so happy to get a "D" in my life. A passing grade -- though barely -- I could move on. The funny thing is, that of all the liberal arts classes in my entire education, this was the one that I learned the most and am happiest I had. Fortunately, the "A's" in my art classes made up the difference for this grade.

I remember looking at colleges and the differences between them. They all had a different emphasis. We first went to Parsons and visited the various buildings on the prospective student tour. I can remember sitting in the office of the administrator pushing the school. I asked if I could see the studios of the students to see the work they were doing. I was informed that that was against the school policy. I was shocked. "What, are you kidding? With how much money is going to be spent, I can't see the studios?" Well, that ended that. I really liked Philadelphia College of Art, P.C.A. I went through the studios and liked the work. We then went to RISD and through the studios and I was blown away. The work was fantastic.

I was in a debate about whether to major in painting or illustration. Looking at the studios in the painting departments was very discouraging. They were all stuck in German Expressionism -- not just RISD -- but all the schools. When touring the studios in the illustration departments, I was thoroughly impressed. The variety was amazing, ranging from traditional painting, to modern Avant-garde, to narrative visual communications. All kinds of mediums were in use, including experimental works and a whole variety of visual expressions that I just didn't see in the other majors. The artwork I saw was just much more exciting.

At RISD, I found the mix that I thought would work for me: Art, art, art, no math and no science. I can complete English requirements with poetry classes. I found the right fit for me. Sophomore year is when everyone goes into his or her major. In the illustration department, you continue classes in drawing, painting and then two illustration courses and a liberal arts course. Drawing and painting was the main focus. Professor Nick Palermo turned out to be my most influential. Figure painting in a fairly traditional manor was his focus. Nick would do elaborate settings for the models. He would bring in tables, chairs, lamps and fabrics. Nick would create a visually appealing setting from which to challenge the artists. He would bounce around the room with his endless energy going from student to student giving his individual critiques. He was demanding of his students and required them to work in his methods. Nick would tease, "After my class, do as you like. During my class, do as I say!"

I took all of Nick's classes and even took two of them twice. I did the same thing for a museum workshop class. It was an eye-opening experience to paint from the masters with my easel set up right next to their painting and copy them brush stroke for brush stroke. I reproduced Corot, Benson and then a Monet. They were excellent exercises.

However, Monet was, again, one of those "light bulb" moments. I spent maybe four of five classes on the painting and would stay late to get it just right. When I finished, it was exact. At RISD you can copy the masters' paintings in the same size as the original. At other museums you must do your copy one-third larger or smaller so there can be no question about the authenticity of the original. When looking at the copy of my Monet next to the original and studying it brush stroke for brush stroke, I found no corrections needed.

At that moment it hits me it's only in one's mind that makes the difference between Monet and me. I can control the paint, the brushes and all the elements of light, color, temperature and texture. All these things I can control to paint anything I want. Now the difficult part begins. I have to figure out what I want to paint and how I am going to paint it stylistically. What steps are needed for me to paint a "Gordon Haas"?

I plugged away at the various RISD courses. At this point, my doing well is not in question. I've built up so many credits, that by the end of my junior year, I was only three credits short of the one-hundred twenty needed to graduate. I took three extra credits each semester, and then during what they called "winter session" when most students took only one course, I always took two. After sophomore year, I even took two courses at a local community college while working full time in the summer -- not for the credits needed -- but, rather, to knock off two liberal arts courses so that I could take more art-related courses at RISD. I knew what a great opportunity I had there and all the sacrifices my parents had made for me. I was going to get the most out of it no matter what.

By the start of senior year, I was ready to be done with school. I guess I was a bit burned out. Senior year was terrific though. Professor David Niles had started a new part of the degree project. This had to do with the business of art and how to promote your work. It also gave guidance on how to deal with art directors, editors, copyright issues, taxes, accounting, pricing -- all the stuff artists don't want to even talk about, let alone deal with. Using the other side of your brain, what a novel thought.

13 THE EARLY YEARS

Illustrating in New York City. I produced a full color print job done of one of my college illustration projects to use as a promotional mailer. In school the professors said, "You need to start doing black and white line illustrations, then two color, then small color spot, then quarter page, then you get to the big full color jobs." The problem was that I didn't do line illustration and I hated doing color separations. What I liked to do was full color. It was a combination of watercolor with glazes of pastel and pastel pencils to pick up highlights. The best work I had was full color.

I spent most of the money I had from washing dishes at a

restaurant the previous summer and got a mailing list together from various resources. I sent three thousand mailers to art directors the week after graduation, mostly in the New York area. It only took about ten days before I got my first call. It was from a national magazine in New York. I head off to meet with the art director with suit, tie, a nicely pressed shirt and portfolio in hand.

I arrive. I'm a bit nervous. While waiting in the lobby, I see that they publish a number of magazines. I meet with the art director and show my portfolio. He quickly flips through the pages looking for consistency while nodding his head up and down. He then hands me the article with the sketch he made and the specs for the job.

My first illustration job is a full color, double page spread with a sixteen-hundred dollar payday. The year is 1984. Right from the get go, I learned a big lesson. If you show full color, that's what you get hired for. If you show line drawings, that's what you will be hired for. Makes perfect "common sense" to me.

This was contrary to what I learned at RISD. It was supposed to be years before I could expect a double page spread like this. I then pulled what black and white work I had at the back of my portfolio out and made it only full color. I feel like I'm starting from scratch in the real world. I have a lot to learn!

I illustrated in New York for about nine years. I was always busy and did quite well, mostly editorial illustrations for magazines, covers for novels and some children's books. After about three years of exclusively illustrating, I started using some of my down time between illustration jobs and started to work in oils again. I always enjoyed it so much that I figured it would be a great use of my time and decided that I should start dealing with galleries and try to sell my paintings.

The more and more I got into the fine art painting, the more it sucked me in. I was having so much fun painting various landscapes and cityscapes. I didn't have my own style of painting at this point but was just mimicking other painters. I needed to find my niche in terms of style of painting. After about six months of studio painting and plein air painting, I made the decision to switch from illustration to fine art. I decided to focus solely on oil painting.

This was a big switch. I had almost no inventory for a gallery to show, let alone sell. I kept my regular illustration clients and also took a job with a newspaper company as a district manager in the circulation department to pay the bills -- I always like to eat. To be strapped for money is no fun.

The newspaper job went from two in the morning until ten in the morning. The rest of the day was mine. For years my sleeping pattern was divided. I slept twice a day from ten p.m. until two a.m. In the afternoon I would have what you might call siesta -- or an afternoon nap of two to three hours. This schedule worked out very well for me. I could get an illustration job in New York with no problem. I could have a daytime appointment or I could go out painting plein air anytime I wanted. Now that I had made the switch to become a fine art painter, I needed to figure out what kind of style to develop.

14 THE EXPERIMENTS

I did a series of paintings on the scene with loose flowing brushwork -- I thought very successful and a lot of fun. The scenes were mostly Sussex County, New Jersey, Steven's State Park, Tillman's Ravine and High Point State Park. These paintings were going in a promising direction, but something at this point in time was missing. I'd spent more hours than I could imagine trying to figure out on how to do "my" paintings once and for all.

I decided that I needed to reconfigure everything that I was doing: the materials I was using, brushes, canvas, paint -- not just materials but also, rather, what I was doing with them. I wrote everything down in a journal to help me analyze every aspect. I had recently finished a new style of painting. For the lack of a better term it could be called "swirlism." I had completed about fifty paintings, often gessoing over a completed painting so I could start again from scratch. Sometimes I would do this five or six times with another change which would lead to another adjustment. Each time something was learned.

Working as a district sales manager for the newspaper company was important at this moment in time for me. I didn't need to rely on money from my painting sales to pay the bills. I used this as my sabbatical time. The galleries were dead. A number of the galleries I had started dealing with were out of business due to the recession. Discerning Images, my best gallery, was gone. Running around with my old style seemed to be a waste of time and energy.

I decided to take as much time as needed to resolve my work and move onto a theoretical approach to my work. If this process takes six months, one year, two years, five years, it doesn't matter. I could cruise in neutral at the newspaper and take all the time I needed. When I started, I hoped it would take no longer than one year. I thought I was being optimistic with predicting one year. I was very pleased it took no longer.

The approach of creating a painting that flickers with light was the general scope of what I wanted to achieve. For the light to bounce off every object, the air all around must be seen. Color must flow from one space to another. It cannot be solid.

I needed to formulate a new method of applying the pigment to cause a flicker. First I changed my medium from the standard mixture of linseed oil, dammar varnish and turpentine to one-hundred percent turpentine. This much thinner medium allowed me to use oils more like watercolors. The purpose of this is to let the oils layer in glazes reminiscent of the Dutch Masters.

With the experimental paintings, I worked with various random patterns in an attempt to achieve the effect I was striving for. Random patterns with lines, dots, swirls, et cetera were tried with mediocre success. The brush patterns were too chaotic for my color theories to work.

After about thirty paintings, the final result was a random swirl pattern. I would use number six round brushes to produce this.

I achieved this by using both hands painting at the same time while swirling in a circular pattern at a forty-five degree angle from each other. This was done with my right hand swirling counter-clockwise and left hand swirling clockwise. Progress is always a process of trial and error.

15 NEW HOPE, PA / LAMBERTVILLE, NJ

I'd been working on my "swirlism" style for a year or so. I'd built up about thirty quality paintings. When I had five paintings, I would approach a new gallery with my work. I had already done the legwork and scoped out galleries that had similar work to mine anticipating that their clientele would also like my work for purchase. Originally I sent slides with no responses or thank you letters. Simply put, all my slides would disappear, never to be seen again. This clearly was not working.

I then decided to make my rounds to galleries on Thursdays and Fridays. I would walk in and ask to see the owner while handing them my slides. If they liked them, I'd offer that I have six or seven originals in my car. If they were interested, I would bring them in. One can only tell the quality of artwork from the original, slides only give an indication of the work. If they thought they could sell them, they would take the paintings on consignment. I would then have another gallery added to my repertoire.

Eventually, I had ten galleries under my belt which averaged five paintings at each, fifty paintings in all. Every six to eight weeks, I would rotate all the paintings at the galleries. The gallery owners loved this because they always had fresh work and things didn't get stale.

One day I got a call from my old friend, Ken Schuyler. Ken was on his way to the "Golden Nugget" and wanted to know if I was interested in exhibiting there also. With paintings in tow, I met Ken at the "Golden Nugget." Upon arrival, I discovered it was a run down flea market. I thought to myself, "What have you gotten me into? This is ridiculous. It's an hour and a half drive back home -- oh, what the heck." They had a little building that served good hot dogs, plus Ken and I could catch up on old times.

Ken and his dad once had a gallery in Upper Montclair, New Jersey, about fifteen miles from New York. Theirs was the first one I exhibited in. Ken and I became lifelong friends. Their gallery went under after about eight years and his dad passed, so I figured it was a nice outing with nothing to lose. We had our java and hung out. I had my paintings. Ken had his prints, etchings and lithographs. It was a beautiful day. I wandered around the huge market. I was greeted with an eclectic array of goods. I arrived back to the area where Ken and I were stationed. Ken was excited about a fellow who had been there but a few minutes ago. He then handed me his card that read, "Doug Reinhardt, gallery director of Genest Gallery, Lambertville, New Jersey." I responded, "I guess I should contact him?" Ken answered, "Oh, no. When we finish here, he wants you to bring your work by the gallery to show the owner."

Late that afternoon, we arrived and I pulled out a couple of paintings. I proceeded to walk through the front door of the gallery. It was a magnificent Victorian building made exclusively of cut stone and fifteen-foot ceilings. I then met Doug. He called over to Bernard Genest, the gallery owner, to inspect the paintings. Bernard then asked if I had more. I responded, "I'll be right back." I then proceeded to fetch more paintings out of my truck. "This is interesting," I thought. I drug them out, one by one, until about fifteen were stacked against the walls of the gallery. They picked out seven that they wanted to keep on consignment. They were also interested in setting up a one-person show. I thought to myself, "That stupid flea market wasn't such a bad idea after all!" You never know what things can lead to. Lesson learned.

My introduction to the Lambertville / New Hope area is now complete. I fell in love with the area: the river, the canals, the local farms, galleries and an eclectic array of shops. I am intrigued. I find that there is a large art community here and a long tradition in all of the arts. I visit the area a number of times -- not just plein air painting, but also as a kayaker. I'd been an enthusiast for a number of years and the river here is beautiful.

With the canals on both sides of the river, I get an idea. I can put my kayak in the canal and paddle my way up north, portage over to the river and make my way back south. This is wonderful. I don't need someone else to go kayaking. If I move down here from the New York area, I would be able to walk outside my home and put my kayak in the canal and go.

The decision is made. I'm moving to New Hope or Lambertville. With twenty-two paintings set for my solo exhibit at the Genest Gallery, I rented a U-Haul and packed up my belongings. I start a new chapter of my life finding a place to call home that gives me a sense of peace.

The exhibit is a success. The space is wonderful. Bernard's clientele is expansive and his public relations is phenomenal. It is the perfect gallery for an artist to show their work. The show ensues and the crowds come in, leaving me pleasantly surprised being that I'm not from this area. The red dots were flying around. There were even two ladies fighting over a painting -- now that's a compliment! Incredibly, at the end of the opening, Doug Reinhardt, the gallery director, went around the room and calculated up the dollar amount for the paintings sold. I was immediately gratified with a check. "Wait, you're kidding me," I thought to myself. Normally receiving a check from a gallery takes at least thirty to sixty days. It was the perfect gallery to be associated with.

Then reality hits. After the exhibit, I head home to celebrate

NO I'M NOT STARVING

the show's success with a glass of wine. Looking at the check just cut to me, I'm rather disappointed with the amount for all the paintings sold. I begin to dissect my cost verses profit. I sit down and run the numbers. Fifty percent to the gallery, twenty-five percent to the I.R.S., the cost of framing plus all other materials -- and I'm not even going to include my time.

Let's say a small painting sells at the gallery for one-thousand dollars. Immediately I'm down to five-hundred dollars with the gallery commission, then twenty-five percent for the Feds. The framing cost is seventy-five. Painting materials cost about fifty and everything else another fifty.

That means for a one-thousand dollar sale at the gallery, I end up with a measly two-hundred in my pocket. Wow. I never really looked at it this way before. While crunching the numbers, what brought it to light for me was seeing the check for all those paintings. To be where I would like to be financially, I would have to have one of these shows every month, ten months a year. I know that will never happen. I look at the check. I look at the numbers. I can't eliminate the I.R.S., we all know that. The biggest chunk is the fifty percent for the gallery. I have to get rid of the gallery commission. The only way I can think of this is to open my own gallery and keep the fifty percent for myself. I will have gallery expenses such as rent, electric, phone and heat. However, I will have my own one-person exhibit seven days a week, three-hundred sixty-five days a year. I pour another glass of wine and decide to start looking for a gallery space in New Hope and Lambertville tomorrow. I sleep well.

The next day I wandered the streets of both towns looking at what was available, the shops and what they sold. I even waited for garbage day and walked around the first thing in the morning with my coffee to see how much garbage was deposited at the curb of each shop. Of course, you have to take into account what type of business it was. A jewelry store is not going to have the volume of garbage that a clothing store has. My first major decision is which town to open my gallery. I'm excited. I feel like I've crossed a line. I'm moving in a direction that is only positive.

I walked into numerous shops on both sides of the river and talked to the shop owners about my desires. I was looking for a small place that I could have a studio in the back and exhibit my work. People were helpful, but I wasn't finding what I was looking for.

I repeatedly wandered around both towns for a number of months checking everything out. I was still working at the newspaper so money wasn't an issue. I could take my time to find the right space. I had decided that Lambertville was the place to be. It was a tourist destination with high quality customers, mostly antiques and art. New Hope was too touristy, too much of the ice cream crowd and tattoo parlors. In the cafés, the Harley Davidson riders would hang out. This is a long-standing tradition in New Hope -- nothing wrong with the Harley riders -- however, I don't think they'll be my customer base.

I'm at a friend's house having dinner and she's talking to her accountant about tax time and setting up an appointment. I then hear her respond, "Oh, you have a space you're renovating." I ask, "Is it residential or commercial?" She relays the information and I find out it's commercial in Lambertville. She then adds that it won't be ready for months. It has to be renovated from residential and brought into code. I offer, "Let me check it out, you never know."

The next week I show up at the appointed time and meet Rick, the new owner of the building. It's a run-down residential building -- and when I say "run-down," I'm not kidding. As I walked in, the floor sunk down six inches on one side of the room. While it was empty, a water leak from the bathroom upstairs caused serious structural issues in the back of the building. As I looked around, it wouldn't be ready for many months. However, the location on Bridge Street was excellent and worth the wait.

I spent quite a bit of time hanging out across the street on weekends to see how the customer flow was. I hung around with my java watching people and watching potential customers to see if they made it to this end of town. I marked on my clipboard how many passed the gallery space and how many turned back towards the center of town. This was a walking town, all looked good

I made an agreement with Rick -- a handshake -- no lease, done the old-fashioned way. I will take the space when it's ready. Time goes by. I'm biding my time at the newspaper. I'm getting many paintings done while the carpenters are rebuilding the space.

As they worked through the process, I had the opportunity to visit with Rick, and we made changes according to our needs. However, there was a problem. With delays in zoning, change of use and township bureaucracy, it took six months longer to get it done than expected.

16 THE GALLERY

It is August 4th 1993, the first weekend. I opened the door and all is set. I have no back up. I don't work for the newspaper company now. I don't do illustration anymore. I have no choice. I have to make it work. I'm in one-hundred percent.

It's kind of strange for me. I paint at my easel set up at the back of my gallery. Mr. and Mrs. McCormick came into the gallery all excited. They start looking and then pick out a painting. I think to myself, "Oh, this is good." To my pleasant surprise they kept looking and started picking out other paintings. In the end, they decided on four paintings. Jim was an engineer and we made a deal, half up front and one-hundred dollars a month until it's paid off. I got a check every month for the next ten months. It was a beautiful thing.

This sale was very important, for one-hundred and eighty-seven reasons. This is what I had in the bank the day the gallery opened. Between getting everything ready for the gallery and the first month's rent, lighting, framing, Visa machine and all the other incidentals, I was broke. With four paintings sold on the first weekend, I hoped this was a sign. No risk, no gain.

Now for the first time in my life, I was a full time "painter." I'm here in my gallery space with my easel and it's all out there. It's just me and the rest of the world. My strategy to make this work is to build time. Building time, I believe, is the key. Time is my enemy. I spend as little money as possible -- scrimping, scrimping, scrimping. My general rule is that I only spend money on something that makes me money. Paints make me money, panels make me money and frames make me money along with rent, electric and telephone. Other than that, I don't need it. I need to keep my doors open and stretch out time. The longer I stretch out time, the longer

I'll be here. The longer I'm here, the more I can paint. The more I can paint, the better I'll get. The better I get, the more I'll sell -- and so on and so on.

With two-thousand made on my first day, I was very pleased. Words can't even describe the emotion and the relief that I made the right decision. Who knows what's in store for the future. For now, I have a start. I have just built in some time. Next month's rent is covered. I am finally an artist making my living as a painter. No one can take that away from me.

I set up at the back of the gallery, and every day I arrive at eight in the morning and paint. It's amazing how much painting one can get done when the only thing to do is paint. I did mostly studio work at this time with the swirlism style. My first year, I'm open every day, seven days a week including Christmas and New Year's -- ok, I left at two o'clock on Christmas. I was determined to make every possible sale and discover the patterns of customers and what I needed to do to make things happen and be successful.

It was a struggle for a while. I sold paintings for far less than they were worth, but when you calculate the fifty percent commission at a regular gallery, they were at a reasonable price. I was moving my work at a consistent pace. The price was right, the quality was there and the public could find me.

The other gallery owners in town knew me before I opened my gallery. Once I opened, they never spoke to me again. We might bump into each other in the bank or at a restaurant, but it was never the same. As far as they were concerned, I was cutting into their livelihood. I had just cut the middleman out. They couldn't compete. They were not happy.

Months go by and I'm still here. I'm painting away and people are coming in and buying my work. I'm able to pay my rent, my heat, electric, et cetera. The numbers show what can happen when you have a one-person show all year long. After some time, I realize that I'm living the dream. I'm a painter who paints what he loves and is making a living at it.

I then look into the idea of printing lithographs to have inexpensive prints at the gallery. I am able to get three lithographs done. They sell well in the gallery, but having only three choices is frustrating. It is far too expensive to have thirty or so printed at one time. It is simply cost prohibitive.

I plug away with my oil paintings, figure drawings and lithographs. I then go to a fellow artist's opening. He puts together a nice show. His subject matter leaves a lot to be desired, as far as I'm concerned. I always find interesting the different philosophies artists have. He is like a photojournalist with a paintbrush. His style is sketchy with some highlights and dabs of color thrown in. I wouldn't really call it "painting." Rather, I would call it sketching with a brush. We are chatting away, and I see on his desk a bowl with a small image of one of his paintings with his name on it. It is a refrigerator magnet. I think to myself, "That's clever." He then tells me that people put them on their fridge, and it's like free advertising. He adds, "You are always reminding them of your work." I comment, "That's a nifty idea. Who does them for you?" He replies, "Oh, I do them myself. I get the magnet stuff from Staples. It comes in full sheets, and I print them on my laser printer." I immediately ask if I can have one.

The light bulb goes off big time. I leave his exhibition with the little refrigerator magnet in my pocket and with the knowledge that I can publish my own prints. I can do my prints in house of any of my paintings in various sizes. I can print everything, and the customers will tell me which ones sell by how many they buy. There is no more guessing and no bad inventory. If it sells, I keep it in inventory. If it doesn't sell, I pull it. With no upfront cost of printing the whole run, I can print on an as-needed basis.

I stare at the little magnet for weeks. The darned thing is not even two inches square. I go online and start researching color laser printers. The technology is still in its infancy. The machines themselves are not that expensive. The inks are where they get you. That's fine with me, because my start up cost is only about two-thousand dollars for the printer. If I'm churning through ink, that means I'm selling the prints, so the ink cost is irrelevant.

My goal is to sell enough prints to equal the amount of my mortgage. It would be like living mortgage free. I decide to standardize everything. I do the research and buy glass, matting and frames in bulk to keep my unit costs down. I get mats precut in two standard sizes. The only thing I have to cut is the foam core backing for the framing. The parts all get shipped to the gallery. I simply take the components and assemble them.

I pick out forty local scenes in two sizes matted and displayed in a clear plastic bag at the retail price of thirty-five dollars and seventy-five dollars. I also offer a selection of various ones framed. I also keep a stock of frames in the back of the gallery. If someone wants one framed differently, I simply send them down the street for a cup of coffee. I tell them, "Give me twenty minutes and I'll have it framed up for you." I cover half my mortgage payment the first month. The second month, I almost make my goal of covering the mortgage. I then realize that I underestimated the potential of this. In the meantime, I'm tweaking the inventory. I begin to see the ones that are becoming the best sellers. I convert many of my paintings that I have from slide to digital. I continuously tweak the inventory. After four months, I sold twice the amount of my mortgage. It takes a couple of years to hit its peak with monthly sales nearly ten times my mortgage.

17 THE CUSTOMERS

When I was first going to open the gallery, I was concerned that I wouldn't like dealing with the customers. I was so used to working in my studio at home that it might be a problem getting disturbed all the time. We are all creatures of habit. One gets used to working a certain way. It turns out that I love dealing with the customers. Not working in a vacuum has improved my painting. I did not expect that to happen. I've even started writing down the comments people would say, good or bad.

My favorite one is when this older couple came into the gallery. They spent quite a bit of time looking around. The fellow then walked up real close to one of my paintings and called his wife over. "Martha, Martha, take a look. It looks like just before my cataract operation."

One of my other favorites is one day when I was sitting in the back of my gallery painting. The front door to the gallery was open. A well-dressed lady, about sixty with large diamond jewelry, popped her head in and asked, "Is this artist dead?" I looked at her, I held up my paintbrush and replied, "Not yet!" She cocked her head slightly, and without a word, pivoted out the door, down the steps and was gone.

Then on other days things like this happen. A man in his thirties came in holding the hand of his young son of about eight years. The boy's jaw dropped open, his eyes wide. While pulling on his dad's shirt, the little boy exclaimed, "Dad, dad, is this Monet? Is this Monet?" I came to find out they visited the Metropolitan Museum of Art in New York the day before. The little boy thought he was in Monet's studio. In the end, though, people's comments mean the same thing, absolutely nothing. A grain of salt and that's about it.

I had been doing juried shows for sometime. They are good for publicity and the commissions are lower than galleries -- about twenty-five percent -- and also good for the resume to justify raising your prices. Here is an example of one painting's journey: I had a horse racing scene receive first place in one exhibition; honorable mention in another; while rejected from slides in another; rejected from submitting the original in another. It was the oldest painting I had and I couldn't sell it -- oh, yes, and did I mention that this painting was exhibited at the Kentucky Derby Museum in an invitational only exhibit? In the end, the painting found its home in Chicago having been sold through an interior design consultant.

There is an old joke about what gets accepted and wins awards at these shows. It depends on what the jurors had for breakfast that morning. Anything can happen. Winning first place and getting rejected mean the same thing, absolutely nothing. I don't care about the awards, the articles in the papers or anything else. All I care about is did it sell. I see the sale of my paintings as the catalyst that gives me the opportunity to do more paintings.

As I am writing this, I am in the midst of getting everything together for our second painting trip to Positano, six weeks this time. Donna has already prepped all seventy panels. If I didn't sell my work, I would never be able to go on a six-week painting trip to Italy. Selling my work is a means to an end. The "end" is to do more painting -- and hanging out in the Amalfi Coast isn't half bad either!

18 CHRISTINE

I met Christine at the coffee shop in town. Christine was collecting donations for a walk she was participating in for multiple sclerosis. Later I found out that I was her largest donation. My attempt at trying to impress her apparently worked.

The coffee shop is where everybody seems to meet in Lambertville. They started in the early eighties as a shop that had a variety of goods. Originally they had a lot of woven fabrics. Lisa, the owner, had looms in the back featuring her handmade rugs. It developed over time into a coffee shop. One day I was at the gallery interviewing someone for the co-op gallery I started on Coryell

Street. In walks Christine in a jaw dropping halter-top. With her yoga shoulders bulging, she asked me out to dinner. We went to a wonderful restaurant in town, Siam's, a great Thai restaurant. The owner / chef is from Thailand. All the restaurants in town are authentic. Ota-ya, the sushi restaurant, is run by a Japanese family; Tortuga's is all Mexican; the French restaurant, Manon -- yes, the chef / owner is from Provence. We are definitely spoiled with the quality cuisine right at our doorstep. We have a great meal at Siam. I always get the appetizer with the peanut sauce -- I'm addicted. Everything just seems right. We walk around town. After a three-hour date -- let's just say the rest is history.

Three weeks later, I ask her if she has ever traveled overseas. Christine went to England a few years ago. I now know she has her passport. This was a leading question in anticipation for asking her to come with me to my exhibition in Laon, France. Heck, I figured if we could survive a vacation together for two weeks, well, maybe we have something here. I got my passport and she's ready with hers. We packed up the paintings and off to France we go. Neither of us has been to France before. As a matter of fact, this was my first trip out of the States. We had a terrific trip. Winging it from place to place and not being locked into a schedule worked out perfect for both of us.

A little over a year later we got married on the canal in New Hope. The canal has been a huge part of Christine's life for years and now it's a part of mine, too. We are both early birds and walk on the picturesque canal that runs along the banks of the Delaware River every morning. Because of the canal's importance to us, we decided to incorporate it into our wedding.

The first canal barge was for the actual service and Champagne afterwards. The second barge was the party boat with food and a jazz band. Donna worked at West End Farm during this time and part of what they offered were carriage rides in New Hope. It was a must to have Christine and her mom arrive in a horse drawn carriage. We had an intimate ceremony before departing down the canal with a Champaign toast. All the guests and the new couple rode on the barge, all the while being pulled by a donkey along the canal path. This created the intimate setting that we were striving to achieve.

Originally we thought we would go to the Caribbean for a

honeymoon. However, we changed our plans when we found -- or I should say Christine saw a picture of a little stone house in a real estate office in town. She showed me the picture. It was a stone house and what looked like a forest around it. The price was in our range. I thought to myself, "Oh, boy. What's wrong with it? Something really big must be wrong for the price to be this good." We asked around at the coffee shop if anyone knew where the street was. We knew it was in Lambertville, but we didn't recognize the street name. A fellow told us he thought it was just south of town and up the hill. We jumped in my jeep to check it out. We found the street and up we went. It was a dirt road that needed a lot of work. There it was, perched on the side of a hill hidden in the woods with a babbling stream a stone's throw away. Now I'm really convinced that the house must be a disaster.

We contacted the real estate office next to my gallery and set up an appointment to see the house. The owner of the real estate office laughed. "You wouldn't even be able to stand up in the living room." I practically had to beg him into letting us see the house.

We drove up a couple of days later with Gene and a fellow

from the listing agent. We spend about an hour and a half perusing the property. I immediately saw why everyone had been scared away from the place. The owner had dropped the price three times in three years. The house was riddled with water problems. The whole house had a musty, damp smell. The entire roof would have to be replaced at some point.

I next explored and found the problem with the water at the back of the house. I came to find it's actually an easy fix. All I would have to do is redirect the water off the roof, problem solved. The water issues were easily remedied without breaking the bank. This old house just needed some tender, loving care.

We made the offer, the owner counters, we counter, she accepts. Maybe we were a little crazy, but we only looked at one house. We knew it immediately when we saw it and that was it. Exactly ten days after the wedding we closed on the house -- nothing like doing everything at once. Needless to say, our honeymoon became a simple five-day retreat to Cape May, New Jersey. Neither of us had been there before. We enjoyed it so much, we returned every August for the next six years.

We set up a workshop in the new living room. The only things we moved over to the new/old house were the tools. We had a plan to get the main floor in a livable state. The idea was so that the living room and the kitchen would be in good shape so we could retreat to them and not always be living amongst a construction project.

The first thing we needed to do was to remove the loft in the living room so that I could stand in the house. People must have been really short back then. This section of the stone house was built in 1704. It was then doubled in size by adding the next stone section in the 1760's. In the 1970's, they added three small rooms of wood construction. Ironically, the newest section is where most of the structural problems were. The stone section -- well, stone is stone -- not much happens to it.

I got the saws-all out and cut out the loft and reused the lumber for various projects. It took about six hours of work and we magically had a cathedral ceiling where once you couldn't stand. Between the kitchen and living room, we tore out a brick and plaster wall so that the kitchen and living room became one large space. I could now cook and interact with our guests. The refrigerator was then tucked discreetly under the staircase. After finding a home for the stove, we were able to enjoy our new kitchen table where before there was none. No one seemed to have a vision for this poor old house.

We spent two months renovating to get the house back to the original flavor. For example, all the floors were brick linoleum with two more layers of floors on top of the original. We tore it all out to get to the wide planked wood floors. That entailed a huge sanding job and tung oil. Now they are beautiful.

Time was marching on and I had to get a wood-burning stove in. It was now the beginning of October and the air was changing rapidly. There is an oil furnace in the house. However, that only heats the newer wood section and the downstairs workshop. The main living space, the living room and the kitchen have no heat. There was, at one time, a wood burning stove. You can see the hole in the chimney where the pipe went in.

A friend of a friend had a Yodel wood-burning stove for sale. It had hardly been used and was a steal for one-hundred and fifty dollars. The only catch was you had to come and get it. It was probably the best buy I ever made. When I went to pick it up, I knew it would be heavy. However, I didn't anticipate the steps I had to get it down. I managed the task somehow by myself -- it must have been the adrenaline. I bought the stove piping from a local fireplace shop and assembled the piping all the way up the chimney and out the top. I wasn't going to trust a three-hundred year-old chimney. We now have the warmest heat one could desire. There is so much wood lying on the ground that much of it rots away before I have a chance to cut it up for firewood. Twelve years later and I still haven't bought a single piece of wood. We are self-sustaining with our five acres' worth of wood on our property.

I built a new platform for the wood-burning stove to sit on. The materials I used were blue stone and Mercer tiles all symbolizing the history of the house. The first tile is a Native American, because it originally was their land. The second is another Native American trading tea -- our house, when first built, was an Indian trading post. The third is an old three-mast sailing ship, which is how our ancestors arrived. The fourth is the harvest, since the hillside behind the house was once a farm. The fifth is a palette symbolizing all the artists who have lived here -- both from the past and now me. Last, but not least, the castle. As we all know, your home is your castle.

This is definitely a "This Old House" project inside and out. We greatly expand the outside eating area. I then built a large arbor that includes new stonewalls. I replaced the rotted railroad tie and brick steps with stone. Our end goal is to make it look like everything is as if you went back in time to 1704. The only telltale sign of today is the electric line at the back of the house, and that's barely visible.

Over the last few years we have added herb gardens so we can enjoy fresh herbs and for making our year's supply of herbs de Provence. A hundred or so basil plants make enough pesto to freeze and use all winter. We have numerous fig trees, olive trees and enough tomato plants for sauces, sun dried tomatoes and, of course, fresh during the season. Not to mention the stonewalled terraced garden. Our Italian-villa-lifestyle in Lambertville is near complete.

Our little house has quite an interesting history. Artists Elsie Driggs and Lee Gatch lived in the house for about thirty-five years.

They were a part of the New Hope School (Modernists). Lewis Stone lived next door, another New Hope Modernist. There was a little enclave of artists here on Weeden Street. James Michener, the writer from Doylestown, was good friends with Lee Gatch. According to Gene Lelie, the local realtor, who, as a young child, hunted in the woods around our house, told us a few stories about Michener and Gatch downing a few too many on our patio. Too bad these three-hundred year-old stone walls can't talk. I would love to hear the stories of when the captains and sergeants of the revolution absconded with our house to set camp all the while planning the battle of Trenton. So many stories of the past lost in history wanting to be told.

19 IT'S A SMALL WORLD AFTER ALL

A woman walks into my gallery. "I read in the newspapers that you've painted in Positano." "Yes," I reply, thinking she might be interested in one of my paintings. She then hands me a mailer and tells me that the mayor of Positano is an artist himself and is having an exhibition at the Peggy Lewis Gallery right here in town. I stare at the mailer in a bit of disbelief. Positano is about the same size as Lambertville, only three-thousand five-hundred people. What are the odds of him having an exhibit only one block away from my gallery?

Ogden Lewis is her name. She explains about her grandmother who, in the 1950's, had a painting workshop school in Positano. I am very surprised that this is the first time I have heard about the workshop. It then hits me. I can't believe it. My friend, Francesco, in Positano had told me about this American workshop that brought the arts to Positano for thirty years. I informed Ogden that I had heard about the painting workshop in Positano, but had no idea that it was the Lewis family from Lambertville.

I relayed a story to Ogden about a lady who came up to me while painting in the upper part of Positano. The woman said something in Italian and I replied, "Inglese?" She then spoke in a British accent and told me about the American workshops that were once here. I found it interesting but had no idea of the connection. Ogden asked me what she looked like. I started describing her and she suddenly blurted out, "That's Ginny." I came to learn that she was the first model for the workshops when they started. Wow. What a small world. I went online and found more information about the workshops. I emailed Francesco, our Italian friend, of this incredible connection between our two little towns. He then emailed me a link to YouTube. I clicked on the link and there is Francesco with the mayor giving out an award to one of the artists that was involved with the workshop all those years ago. Francesco is in attendance to be the interpreter for the mayor. There are many Americans there in the audience including Ogden and her sister, Nora.

This new information gets me thinking about doing my own workshop in Italy. Why not? I have all the tools to do it. I had already been talking to a couple of artists who have their own galleries about opening a joint gallery in Positano. The four of us are all on board. A gallery and workshops in Italy, I like this. In talking with Tony, one of the other artists who had been to Positano in the past -- he's actually the one who first came up with the idea of a gallery in Positano. He said it best, "What are we going to do, wait until we're eighty?"

Francesco turned out to be our go-to-guy in Italy. He will be our eyes and ears. Francesco found us possible spaces to rent. It would be easy for me to transition into a gallery, already having sixty-plus paintings from our time spent in Positano. We then decide to first do the workshop so the other artists can paint in Positano and prepare for the gallery.

Having checked things out with the Italian consulate in Philadelphia, I learned there are twenty-one different types of work Visa's for Italy -- those Italians are famous for their bureaucracy!   I also came to learn that you can't stay in Italy for more than ninety days and still be considered a tourist. The other criteria is that you cannot be employed by an Italian company. In the literature and on their web site they use the word "work" when they actually mean "employed." Doing the workshops and bringing Americans over, I only need my passport and that's it.

With a gallery there are all kinds of bureaucratic problems such as the VAT tax -- i.e., Value Added Tax. I'd been talking with Francesco about him putting the gallery in his name. He would deal with all the bureaucracy and the four of us would send him the artwork to sell, and hopefully we would all make some money. Since I would get paid in Euro, I could just have a bank account over there and let the money accumulate like a rainy day fund. Who knows, maybe someday buy a little place with it?

Tony LaSalle took a trip to Montalcino and Positano this

summer for a month. He was on sabbatical from his teaching job. Collette and Ty -- the two other artists joining Tony and I on this gallery adventure -- will be in Positano during the workshop I set up for October. Kiki and I will arrive in early September for a six-week painting trip.

All the pieces for a gallery in Italy were coming together. I have been thinking of doing workshops at various locations in the spring in Tuscany, Venice, maybe Greece and St.Tropez. Fall each year, in the beginning of October, would be reserved for Positano. This means that Kiki and I would spend a total of three months in Europe each year painting away.

I would be able to sell paintings and prints on both continents. That would be -- as my son says -- "SWEET!" I'm trying to set everything up to be as simple as possible. I want to paint with no worries with Francesco running the day-to-day business in Positano while I'm in the States, and Donna running the day-to-day business in Lambertville while I'm in Italy. This would be a lifestyle that Kiki and I would really enjoy, and I believe painting wise would be best for me. This is something I could see doing for the rest of our lives, as long as we are able to. I'm forty-six now and my parents are healthy right now at eighty-three. If I'm as blessed as they are, that means with a little luck thrown in, it could be thirty-six more years of traveling and painting. That works for me!

20 POSITANO REVISITED

We are currently getting ready for another trip to Positano. There is the painting part, the workshop part, and the gallery part. This, I believe, will be the most exciting trip of all. We have never revisited a place that we have been to before. We know people in Positano, and I'm sure we'll get to know more. We will contact the Mayor and his wife, Vincent, the toy maker down at the beach, and the folks at the Mediteraneo Restaurant. On our last trip, we ate at the Mediteraneo numerous times and became friends with the owner, Enzo, who exhibits many of the local artists. It's kind of strange that we have friends in Italy, but we do!

I'm bringing seventy panels this time. It may be a little too ambitious, but if I don't have the panels I can't do the paintings. I plan to concentrate on views of the Duomo, the beach with the boats, the cafés, street scenes and the lemon trees. I am also going to bring a small sketchbook this time, so when we are hanging out in the cafés I can do some sketching. I haven't done that in years.

We get Chongo ready for the trip. He already has the microchip in him from before. His shots need to be up to date, and he needs to get a check up within ten days of the trip. We are becoming expert packers by now and off we go for a second trip to Positano.

Here we go. We're at the airport and it looks like we are going to beat a hurricane coming up the east coast -- well, maybe, maybe not. We get on the plane on time. So far so good. Chongo is settling in under the seat in front of us. Then the captain of Alitalia makes an announcement in Italian. I can tell it's not good. Here comes the English version. The east coast corridor to Europe is shut down. We are thirteenth in line on the runway. They are parking the plane, and we will be notified when he has further information. He parks and shuts the engines off. There goes the air conditioner. It's raining out very hard and extremely windy. The plane gets hotter and hotter. Chongo is getting uncomfortable and cranky for the first time on a trip. He is hot in the Sherpa bag under the seat. We now have been sitting here for two hours. We are all hot and cranky now.

Finally the captain gets on the horn and lets us know that the corridor has been opened up. However, we are thirteenth so it will be another half an hour before we take off. Maybe we can make up some time on this leg of the flight. If we don't, we won't make our connection to Naples from Rome. After eight hours the flight starts to wind down and it looks like we might make our connection. With the tailwind and the pilot hitting the gas, we made up quite a bit of time. We finally land and all looks good -- oops, here we go again. The pilot informs us he pulled up to the wrong gate. Please stay seated. We are waiting for a tow to take us to the proper gate. Needless to say, we miss our connecting flight.

Christine and I console each other in that so far this trip is not going very well. They reschedule us for another flight to Naples. It leaves in four hours. I then have to contact Francesco because he is arriving with a driver in Naples to pick us up. My phone, with the new global roaming, won't work -- oh, great! To our rescue, a very nice fellow in the airport offers the use of his phone and we get everything worked out. Eventually, we make it to Positano and our villa at Il Gabbiano -- very late and very tired, but we make it with the whole trip in front of us.

On the ride from the airport, Francesco tells us that the bookstore is available for rent. The owner of the bookstore is in the process of moving out. Francesco had already spoken to the owner of the building and we have first dibs on the space. However, we must move fast if we are to get it. With a space that great, it won't be around for long.

I'm a bit surprised. I wasn't expecting things to move so fast. Last year a space fell through. I had heard from Francesco in emails about the possibility of this bookstore opening up, but it was just in the wind with no timetable -- let alone immediately. I was in the frame of mind to paint and nothing else. This was from left field. Francesco had been keeping an eye out for spaces. However, I wasn't expecting this just off the plane.

Christine and I got a good night's sleep and the first thing in the morning after our cappuccino, we took a stroll by the "gallery" space. It's obvious that work was needed inside and out. However, from what I can tell, it's all cosmetic. The location is excellent. The space is just up the street from the Le Sirenuse, the most expensive hotel in town, and a few steps from the bus stop to Amalfi. There are also numerous high end hotels in the surrounding area. This is an extremely well traveled walking part of Positano.

I contacted Francesco to let him know what I thought of the location and to make arrangements to meet with the landlord to get inside and see the place to go over any changes necessary. The arrangements were made for later in the week, so off I go to paint my heart out. I started painting ferociously. It wasn't like my struggle the first trip here. I slipped right into it as if I'd never left. It was so comfortable. It took me some time on the first trip here to get used to the light, but now it's like my second home.

We meet with Raimonda with regard to the gallery space. "Raimonda" is the Italian name for Raymond in the feminine. In Italian, apparently all names have their masculine and feminine version, ending in "O" for masculine and ending in "A" for feminine. We soon came to find out that she owns about ten percent of the entire town. Her grandparents came from England in the 1890's and bought numerous properties for a song. Back then Positano was just a poor fishing village with difficult access in and out. I could just hear the locals back then, "Why do you want to buy another building? It's just a bunch of rock and concrete. We have rock and concrete everywhere. Are you crazy?" Now she is laughing while she owns fortunes in real estate.

We were able to get the five-cent tour of the gallery space. The front of the space facing the street is all glass. The door and windows show the interior of the gallery beautifully. Lit up at night, it will be continuous advertising. The main room is about eighteen by twenty feet. It has a domed arched ceiling that provides ample show space. There is a downstairs room that can be used for shipping, storage and inventory.

We came to an agreement on price and terms and all was set except for one thing: I had to contact the other three artists to get them on board. I contacted Colette Sexton first. I did it via text message. I think she was as surprised as I was that it came up so fast. Colette, Tony, Ty and I had gotten together prior to the trip to talk about the possibility of starting a gallery in Italy. We had gone over all the ins and outs. There was also a possible gallery space the year earlier that fell through. We figured that we would have plenty of time. The sudden change of events was a surprise to everyone.

Colette contacted everyone else and they decided to get together at her house to discuss the gallery. I started receiving various text messages and then phone calls with everyone's concerns, thoughts and ideas. There were lots of logistical problems to work out, such as alternating schedules for who will be manning the gallery during the high season. Not to mention all the financial details to be divided between the four artists and Francesco. Colette and Ty had never even met Francesco. It was an easy decision for me. However, it's a huge leap of faith for the others. This was a large financial commitment -- not just with the gallery -- but there was also the travel and cost for each artist to stay at the gallery for six weeks each high season. We had to take into account any loss of income back at our galleries in the States.

Collette, Ty and Tony had their pow-wow, and came in with

thumbs up. It took a little cajoling with one of the artists. However, I reminded him of something he told me in the beginning, "What are we going to do, wait until we're eighty?" With that, Tony is the last to take the plunge.

I gave the word to Francesco that we are all on board. Now the hard part begins. I didn't realize at first how much bureaucracy that I would have to deal with. In the beginning, everything seemed to be running smooth. I even had emails from my son, Dillon, with responses to our progress, "Wow, you're really moving through the Italian red tape quickly."

Well, it started off just fine. I dropped off the information to the accountant. Some paperwork needed to go to Amalfi. We then needed copies of everyone's passport. Colette faxed them to the accountant. Next we needed an Italian-to-English translation of the business agreement and the lease for everyone including the notaries in Amalfi.

The notaries are a big deal here. They are sort of a cross between a lawyer, accountant and county clerk. We all meet at the Notary office in Amalfi for the big meeting to get the paperwork completed so we can open the gallery bank account and apply for the credit card machine. Colette, Ty, and myself are there. Ty is our chauffeur with his car along the Amalfi Coast. Colette is feeling a bit woozy from the wildly curvy drive. We arrive and meet Francesco in the main square. "Ciao." "Ciao." Francesco is dressed in what he called his "costume." Indiana Jones would be proud. He is in his hiking gear to the hilt, having just completed a day's hike with a tour group. Francesco guides us up a strange set of steps adjacent to the main square in Amalfi. If you didn't know just where the steps were you would never find them. We meet with the interpreter in the waiting room. We then came to learn that to form the limited liability company, we can do nothing since Tony is not here. We have all of his information from the accountant, passport, et cetera, but that doesn't mater.

Francesco then disappears into the other room with the powers that be. We hear the typical yelling and screaming that is the Italian way. Francesco deals with them in ways that we can't due to the language barrier and cultural differences. We move forward with the three of us that are here. As a result, Tony is dropped from the paperwork until he returns next summer.

First the Notary has to read the business certification in Italian and then in English. He reads very slowly, while sitting behind his eight-foot long desk, as big and pompous as possible. The interpreter was dissecting everything all the while a second interpreter clarifies what the first interpreter is doing. You then have two witnesses plus the other ladies that worked in the office. There must have been about twelve of us in the room. A lot of people wasting a lot of time. This whole process in Italy took about six weeks. Francesco said it best, "This is all to justify the fee." In total, about two-thousand two-hundred Euro or about three-thousand five-hundred dollars at the current exchange rate. This was all to get the business number for the VAT tax and to open the bank account and get the Visa machine.

In the States, the same process takes about two hours at the county clerk's office filling out a few forms for state sales tax. The two hours would include plenty of time for a cappuccino break. The cost totals a whopping thirty-five dollars for everything. In Italy, it's one-hundred times the cost and time to do the same thing. I just kept saying to myself, "I only have to do this once, I only have to do this once."

On the fourth week of our trip, we do the workshop. It is a plein air excursion all around Positano. We were basically reconstituting the "Positano Art Workshop." Colette and I taught this one. I would teach from nine until noon, and then Colette would teach from three until six. The students would then be able to have a siesta in the middle of the day, perhaps go to the beach or hang out in a café. Wednesday was reserved for touring around. It was a day to grab your camera and see the sights. Some of us went to Capri and others to Ravello. Some were a bit exhausted from the painting schedule and decided to take a boat ride to a private cove and get a little sunbathing in.

There were seven painter-students plus various spouses and significant others on the trip. That made for about a dozen folks we brought over to enjoy a little slice of paradise. Colette and Kevin were able to stay for eighteen days in Positano with no hotel bill. The workshop covered the bill. Christine and I had gotten about the same amount of time covered with our apartment bill. We stayed for a total of forty-four days. Colette and I divided the revenue from the workshop equally between us and put it towards our stay.

The first morning of the workshop we met at nine a.m. in front of the hotel. Off we went to one of my favorite spots to paint. It's just up and around the bend. It has one of the best views looking down the Amalfi coast with the Duomo and the beach in view.

The artists did great paintings during their workshop week. We took some of the artists out on a trial run prior to the trip. We went to Washington's Crossing State Park to set up our plein air painting equipment. Everyone works in different mediums: oils, watercolors, pastels, et cetera. I wanted to do a trial run so that there were no surprises once we got to Italy. The oil painters can't bring turpentine on the plane. I will get turpentine at the hardware store in Positano and have a supply for everyone. Christine and I will be in Positano for two weeks after the workshop so any students' wet paintings will have time to dry and we can bring them back in our luggage.

Italy is a fabulous place to visit. The food is fantastic and the warmth of the people make you feel like you're a part of their family. However, you must understand, when getting things done, they work on what I call "Italian time." The process for opening the gallery had taken so long in getting the paperwork finished from Amalfi and Salerno that after six weeks we had to leave for home in a few days. Raimonda was unreachable by landline, cell or otherwise. With time running out, we had no choice but to get into the gallery space to ready it for business. We also needed to get in to set up all the artwork. I left twenty-five paintings. Ty and Colette each had done about ten paintings and brought a variety of prints from home. I had about forty-five prints that Donna shipped through DHL, enough work to fully stock the gallery.

I told Francesco to leave a message for Raimonda that we had to switch from Italian time to New York time. We were leaving in a couple of days and had no choice. In two days, we finished everything and Francesco was all set thanks to Kevin, Collette's husband, who did the work of pulling out shelving, clean up, spackling and painting. We hadn't even signed the lease, and I sold a print and an oil painting before we officially opened. We packed and off we went, another trip finished with much accomplished: fifty-four paintings completed, the workshop and a second gallery abroad. And "No, I'm not starving." Ciao!

ABOUT THE AUTHOR
GORDONHAAS.COM

Gordon wrote this book to share his experiences in making a living as a full-time artist. The hope is that other painters, sculptors or anyone interested in the arts will get a better understanding of one's journey into becoming a professional artist.

Made in the USA
Charleston, SC
04 March 2013

The Case for Christ

A Journalist's Personal Investigation of the Evidence for Jesus

Lee Strobel

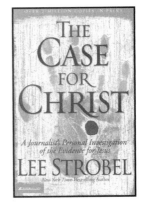

Using the dramatic scenario of an investigative journalist pursuing a story, Lee Strobel uses his experience as a reporter for the *Chicago Tribune* to interview experts about the evidence for Christ from the fields of science, philosophy, and history. Winner of the Gold Medallion Book Award and twice nominated for the Christian Book of the Year Award.

The Case for Faith

A Journalist Investigates the Toughest Objections to Christianity

Lee Strobel

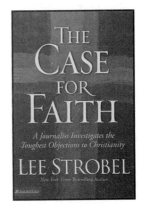

This eagerly anticipated sequel to Lee Strobel's bestselling *Case for Christ* finds the author investigating the nettlesome issues and doubts of the heart that threaten faith. Eight major topics are addressed, including doubt, the problem of pain, and the existence of evil.

Becoming a Contagious Christian
Communicating Your Faith in a Style That Fits You
MARK MITTELBERG, LEE STROBEL, AND BILL HYBELS

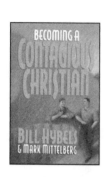

We all want to reach lost people for Christ. But the truth is, most Christians never lead another person to Christ.

Becoming a Contagious Christian is designed to help change that. This best-selling course provides all the tools you'll need to help your church's members discover their own personal styles of evangelism. In only eight 50-minute sessions, you can help people learn to comfortably and confidently communicate their faith. Taught in twenty languages around the world, this course is designed especially for people who think that evangelism is not for them.

Now help every member of your church develop the heart and skills for reaching lost people. They can't all be Billy Graham—but they can be exactly who God designed them to be!

The curriculum kit (0-310-50109-1) includes:
One Leader's Guide (0-310-50081-8), one Participant's Guide (0-310-50101-6), Overhead Masters (0-310-50091-5), and the Drama Vignettes Video (0-310-20169-1)

Also available:
Becoming a Contagious Christian, Youth Edition (see page 409).
The entire curriculum has been rewritten for high school students, complete with a new Drama Vignettes Video containing situations and actors they can relate to.

Becoming a Contagious Christian
The original book by Bill Hybels and Mark Mittelberg
Hardcover 0-310-48500-2
Softcover 0-310-21008-9
Audio Pages 0-310-48508-8

ZONDERVAN™

GRAND RAPIDS, MICHIGAN 49530 USA

WWW.ZONDERVAN.COM

WILLOW
Willow Creek Resources